How To Get Your Book Published

How To Get Your Book Published

Dr. Samuel C. Gipp Th. D.

DayStar Publishing
PO Box 464 • Miamitown, Ohio 45041

Copyright, 2003
Dr. Samuel C. Gipp Th. D.

No part of this book may be reproduced either in printed form, electronically or by any other means without the express written permission of the author. Said letter of permission must be displayed at the front of any electronically reproduced file.

(Think about it! You spend years writing a book and **thousands** of dollars to have it printed. You then rent warehouse space for them until they're sold. Then somebody puts it on the Internet and it gets copied free of charge. **It's not a question of getting rich!** If the books don't turn a profit, no more books can be written and all the books are rotting in some warehouse.)

ISBN 1-890120-20-0

Library of Congress No.

2003116678

Books by this Author

* The Answer Book
* An Understandable History of the Bible
* A Practical and Theological Study of The Gospel of John
* A Practical and Theological Study of The Book of Acts
* A Practical and Theological Study of The Book of Romans
* Living With Pain
* Answers To the Ravings of a Mad Plunger
* Job
* Reading and Understanding the Variations Between the Critical Apparatuses of Nestle's 25th and 26th Editions of the *Novum Testamentum-Graece*
* How To Minister To Youth
* Selected Sermons (Vol. 1 - 10)
* Life After Y2K
* For His Pleasure
* Character Studies in the Old Testament
* How To Get Your Book Published
* (Christian School materials)

Contents

Preface i
Introduction ii

Part One: How to Get Your Book Printed
1. Writing your book 2
   - Informative 2
   - Educational 3
   - Historical 4
   - Fiction 4
   - Humor 5
   - Poetry 6
   - **Tips on Writing** 6
     - A word on grammar 8
   - **Tips on Formatting** 10
     - Justification 10
     - Footnotes 11
     - Type Styles 13
     - Widows & Orphans 14
     - Page Layout 14
     - Page Headers 16
     - Page Numbering 17
     - Text Box 18
     - Pages other than text 19
     - Proofreading 23
   - **Cover Design** 23
     - Front Cover 23
     - Back Cover 24
     - Spine 24

Necessary Numbers..**25**
    ISBN number...**25**
        Library of Congress number.....................25
        Bar Code..26
Copyright..**27**
What about the money?....................................**28**
    The expense of printing and publishing.................28
    The money you will make......................................31

2. What's the difference between "printing" and "publishing"?...........37
    Printing...37
    Publishing..37
What you need to get a book PRINTED..................**38**
    You need a computer......................................38
    You need a laser printer................................38
What's a "book" and what's a "booklet"?...........**38**
    What is a booklet?...39
    What is a book?...39
Steps to the Printer...**39**
    Finished draft...39
    Proofreading..40
    Formatting..40
    Cover..41
At the Printer...**42**
    Kill the dream!..42
    How many books should I have printed?............43
    But it gets worse!...44
Using your Head...**44**
    Money..44
    Realistic sales estimates.................................45
How much should you charge per book?..............**46**
    Hidden costs..47

Part Two: DayStar Publishing: A New Concept in Publishing
3. What DayStar Publishing IS...53

The need for DayStar...53
An idea is born...54
What IS DayStar?..56
   DayStar is a company...56
   DayStar is a publishing company.........................57
   Legitimate Offerings..57

4. What DayStar Publishing ISN'T.................................59
DayStar Publishing ISN'T Buildings......................59
DayStar Publishing ISN'T a Bank..........................59
DayStar Publishing ISN'T a Guarantor of sales......60
DayStar Publishing ISN'T a Conglomerate...............60
DayStar Publishing ISN'T Disconnected..................61
DayStar Publishing ISN'T Greedy...........................62
DayStar Publishing ISN'T for Everyone..................62

Part Three: What can DayStar Publishing do for You?

5. Assistance With Printing..64
How DayStar can help...64
   Contacts...64
   The DayStar Logo....................................65
   ISBN number..65
   Library of Congress number....................65
What about the copyright?....................................66

6. Assistance With Publishing..67
How do I get my book approved?.............................67
   Submitting a manuscript copy..................67
   Submitting a floppy or CD.........................67
   Submitting cover graphics.........................67
What happens if my book is approved?.................67
What next?..70
   Re-approval..70
Into the DayStar Publishing catalog.....................71

7. Assistance With Distribution......................................73

DayStar's part in distribution 73
    Distribution to bookstores..73
    Individual sales...74
Your part in distribution 74
Flexibility first..75

8. What Should You Do Now? 76
  Start writing!...76
    Contact DayStar Publishing....................................76
    Don't Contact DayStar Publishing..........................76
  If you're not an author...77
    A worthy cause...77

Appendix 79
Index 93

Preface
Kill the Dream!

Most people who wish to publish a book have a "dream" of what the process is about. So did I when I first started writing.

First, you think that what you are writing about is of the utmost importance and desperately needs to be told. You, of course, are just the person to tell it.

Secondly, you figure that you will write your book and send it off to some big publishing company. They will read it and **love it**. Then they will excitedly contact you asking for permission to publish it for you, **at their expense**. They will do so and the book will become a best seller. You, reluctantly, will be forced to accept wealth and fame. This is the same dream every hopeful movie-star-to-be has. They hope to be at the right place at the right time and be "discovered."

Although both of the above scenarios **have** indeed taken place at some time, they are not the **normal** way that the process works. Most publishing companies, Christian or otherwise, are interested in how much money a book will make for them. This is **not** a condemnation of them, it is just a fact of life. They will not be impressed by either your urgency or glassy-eyed stare.

Getting your book published will be far more difficult than getting it printed. It will require time, effort and money on your part. The sooner you "kill the dream", the sooner you can get started with the **reality** of getting your book published.

Introduction

Many people aspire to be writers. Quite frankly, some shouldn't even try. They have nothing to offer. They simply feel that the world needs to hear their ramblings. Fortunately, getting a book printed and **in circulation** is usually both difficult and expensive enough to discourage them.

But there are some folks who definitely need to be heard. Unfortunately, they face the same hurdles as the afore mentioned group.

I don't know which group you're in. But I have written this book in an effort to make the arduous task of printing **and publishing** a book a little bit easier. I would like to think that some of the questions you have will be answered within these pages.

There will be no "legalese" spoken here. This is being written so that you can understand it. It will be straight forward and helpful. **You need to read this entire document.** There are surely some questions you need answered. But there is other information that you are unaware of that you need to be informed of and will not learn if you confidently ignore what you **think** you don't need. You may not like everything you read but it will help you in the long run and can save you much grief and woe.

Part One:

How to get your book printed

1
Writing Your Book

Why did you write your book?

Informative

Most books have some small educational benefit. Some are aimed directly at teaching. Others have an incidental value in that while reading them, people will learn something that they previously did not know. These books are informative books. Many authors will use this truth to teach something they wish to impart to their readers without openly addressing an issue.

Thus, the "bottom line" on why you wrote your book boils down to one simple statement. Basically a book's author is telling his reader: "Following is proof of
1. Why I'm right; and
2. Why you should be just like me."

Now think about it. If you didn't think your approach to the subject you wrote about was correct, you wouldn't have written your book. If you didn't think that more people needed to understand the subject as you do and arrive at the same opinion, you wouldn't have written your book. So basically all authors think they are right and want to influence people to think as they do. Please, take no offense. No charge has been made against you. No one ever wrote a book and said, "I'm wrong in what I'm saying. Please ignore what I've written." It isn't a sinful act of pride to think you are right. I know of no one who lives under the assumption that everything he believes is wrong. If you thought what you believed was wrong, you would correct it. **Then you'd think you were "right" again!** And then you'd write a book telling people how to be as right as you are.

What you want to avoid is a "high and mighty" view of yourself. No one likes to be around someone who is arrogant or thinks he is better than those around him. If you write in such a manner, it is because that is the view you have of yourself and your readers. **It is a heart issue!** You had better get down on your knees and address and correct it now.

Most books fall into this "Informative" group. They are written to enlighten readers to some truth that they will benefit from knowing. These would include Bible commentaries, ministerial helps, self-helps, and most others.

Educational

Educational books are directed expressly at teaching a particular truth. They should be suitable for a classroom environment. They should be written in as simple a style as the subject affords. Don't assume your readers already know a great deal about your subject or that they will immediately understand the terminology that is unique to your subject. Walk them through the basics of your subject and clearly explain the nomenclature of any symbols involved in defining the material to be examined. It may be helpful to format the book with a wide margin so the students can make notes in the book itself.

Historical

There is much of history that is being rewritten to portray a past that simply did not exist. This is called "revisionist history" and should be a punishable crime. Therefore, due to interest, experience, or just love of the subject, you may wish to write a book to convey what you feel has not been understood clearly by the public at large.

Fiction

This is the field that is the most popular and yet has the most potential for trouble. People have concepts of fiction that are truly **all fiction**! We are all aware of popular fiction writers such as Tom Clancy, Louis L'Amour, W. E. B. Griffin, and Janet Oke. Because of the success and popularity of such writers, the public at large has an almost irreparable misconception of writing. Computers, while they have made the job of writing easier for those who have something legitimate to offer the public, have also given these dreamers a hope that is much larger than their writing ability deserves. Some can work wonders with formatting, graphics, and cover design and yet have nothing of substance in their text.

Today's potential writers tend to spend a lot of time in a fantasy world concerning their own writing ability and their chances of becoming the next Tom Clancy. When you have **nothing to offer**, you can always make up a story. Some of these fabricators have become famous, as already mentioned. Most have not. Why? Because their stories aren't as interesting to others as they are to themselves. Beware of letting your imagination take you farther than you should go. Some feel that the more sensational they can be, the better their chance of success. Okay, you win. **Go set yourself on**

fire! That's pretty sensational!

Beware of the current trap of "realism." Many authors have infested their books and insulted their readers by dragging them into the depths of filth and degradation in the name of "realism." They will use the foulest of language and portray the most depraved of bedroom scenes (**none** are justified) and then, if a cry rises against their tasteless abuse, they will cry, "I was only trying for realism." It isn't "realism" they were really interested in. Think! How many general books do you find that show people **praying**? What? Are you going to claim that people don't pray? Of course they do. Don't claim that prayer is a "private" matter. You are being dishonest. How many people **pray** in their bedroom as well as do anything else some "garbage man" author might wish to picture? These authors **are not** interested in "realism" or they would show some broken-hearted or fear-filled character in the book actually beseeching God to help him. But it isn't "realism" they are truly interested in. They are **really** interested in forcing as much filth, vile language, and sex on their reader as possible. Then, if they are accosted for their transgression, they run to the "artistic liberty" of "realism." The only thing "real" here is their own twisted imagination. The less you have to offer your reader, the more you will want to turn to filth.

Humor

There is a pressing need for clean humor in a world trained by the entertainment industry to think that humor is found written on the bathroom wall of some freeway gas station. **Real humor** takes a great deal of thought. Just compare any of the material generated by the comedy teams of the '30's, '40's, and '50's to the repulsive vomit spewed out by the so-called comedians dredged from the sewer and placed before a crowd on HBO.

True humor lifts hearts and lightens burdens. It is extremely difficult to laugh and feel sad at the same time. True humor is carefully thought out rather than a torrent of four letter words by some imbecile who looks at the crowd following such an assault on their intelligence with a mindless expression on his face that begs, "Don't you think I'm cute?" No! You're **not** "cute." You're vile and repulsive and lack the mental capability to be **really** humorous, so you'll settle for off-color. No talent is needed for such onslaughts.

Poetry

Almost everyone has written a poem or two at some time. That doesn't make him a poet and doesn't automatically bestow desirability on his words. Yet there are some well-thought poems which convey a deep meaning with the twist of their words and depth of their thought.

Tips on writing

The best mind set to have when writing is that you are sitting and talking to your reader. In this manner you will find that you will try to use words and phrases that are easy to understand.

Beware of the standard writer's pitfall! Some authors long to be known as "scholars." Their sole purpose for writing is to allow mere mortals to view their great intellect.

Therefore, they use long sentences and difficult words, thinking that the reader will be impressed by their deep grasp of the English language. **Don't count on it!** Instead, their readers will **curse them** for not being plain spoken.

Supposedly you wrote your book to enlighten your readers to some truth that has not been explained to your satisfaction to this point. You should write, not to the illiterate or child, but to the common man. Don't use words that the common man will not be familiar with. Understandably, there may be some technical necessity for certain words. But if at all possible, use words that will not force your reader to consult a dictionary in hope of figuring out what you're trying to say.

Also, beware of the natural tendency to make a subject more difficult than it really is so that you can make your explanation seem that much more profound. When you know little and have even less to offer your reader, there is a natural desire to overinflate the pitfalls of the subject you are discussing so that your efforts to explain it properly are viewed as heroic.

Many years ago I spoke with a young man who had been a student of mine in a college in which I had taught. He was bright, friendly and intelligent. He aspired to be a writer and wanted me to review something he had written about prayer. He asked me to tell him what I thought of it.

I took the paper to my hotel room and read it that night. He equated prayer to exercising. Just as you don't just start exercising without a proper warm-up, he gave a series of prayer "warm-ups" that needed to be performed before you actually "got down to business" and prayed.

At breakfast the next morning he asked me what I

thought of his dissertation. I told him, "Until I read this, I **thought** I knew how to pray." I then told him, "The **simplest** thing for a Christian to do is to speak to his Father. You took the simplest thing I can do and made it difficult. He is no great man who takes the **simple** and makes it **difficult**. The great man takes the **difficult** and makes it **simple**."

When you write you should endeavor to be as plain and as understandable as you possibly can be. Maybe your readers will not be overwhelmed by an intellect that they fail to see because of your plainness. But they will thank you for making a difficult subject easy for them to understand. It really boils down to what your **real** goal is.

A word on grammar

Most computers have a grammar program with which you can double-check yours. I do not check my writing with a grammar program. There are several reasons why I ignore this opportunity to be grammatically infallible.

1. I am a product of public education. I will gladly blame my gaffs on them since they are also the folks who sabotaged my mathematical skills with "New Math." many decades ago.

2. There are two verses in Scripture which I am certain will not pass the test of a computer grammar program. One of these is Hebrews 11:5, which repeats the word "translate" in some form three different times. The other is Jude 15, where the word "ungodly" appears four times. Both of these verses would fail due to the "redundant" usage of these words. Well, I figure if **the Bible** can't pass a grammar program, then either the grammar program or the Bible has to be my absolute authority. Since I made the decision years as to what my final authority would be, the grammar program is **out**.

3. No matter what you are told about "proper grammar," there really are no rock-hard rules. Somewhere in some huge conference room out there in "Never-neverland" a group of floating brains meets periodically and **changes** the rules. These changes are then sent out through education and the News Industry. We **used** to say, "The data **is**...," then the floating brains decreed that "Data is **plural**"; from then on, we were ordered to say, "The data **are**...." We **used** to say, "The News Media **is**..." (a bunch of intolerant, liberal, murderous...oops! Excuse me; I was on "automatic pilot"). Then the floating brains decreed, "News Media is **plural**," and from then on we mere mortals were ordered to obediently say, "The News Media **are**...."

Furthermore, these grammatical gurus have even made running changes in the spelling of many words. We used to spell "worshipping" with two "p's." Then we were told, "It shall now be spelled 'worshiping' with **one** 'p.'" (Even now my word processing program is screaming at me that "worshipping" is misspelled.) I simply refuse to jump every time some group, that no one can seem to identify, demands that the entire language be altered on **its whim**. It is with great disdain and satisfaction that I disregard their authority. After all, they happily disregard the authority of Scripture, so it is only fitting...er...fiting...fittting that we not take their finite brains too seriously.[1]

---

[1] Remember, as a rule the "gods" who control our language are liberals who will **always** put the defense of one of their fellow liberals **above** good grammar. That is why, many years ago, when **liberal** president

How To Get Your Book Published

Please understand, I am not inviting...invitting...utter chaos. I am simply taking **my message** more seriously than their authority. But keep in mind that you cannot afford to write your book to a "Beverly Hillbillies" level. So you should be reasonable in your writings to be as grammatically correct as possible.

Tips on formatting

Once you are finished writing your book, you will either have it typeset by someone or you will do it yourself. With the advent of computers and high quality word processing programs, formatting has been easy enough for most people to do themselves. Most people who typeset their own work do so for economic reasons. If you are doing your own typesetting, there are some things that can help the look of your finished product.

1. Justification

The type on a page can be "justified" in four different ways. Each type is described below in a short paragraph that is justified in the style mentioned.

1. Centered -
This **centers** the type and lets the space at the right and left

---

Franklin D. Roosevelt misspoke and said "normalcy," which **isn't** a word, the liberal press, rather than condemn their fellow traveler, simply **inserted it into the glossary of proper English**. These are the same folks who condemned vice president Dan Quayle for spelling "potato" with an "e" on the end of it. They are far more interested in **politics** than good grammar and I refuse to pay homage to their politics!

margins change with the differing length of each line. This style is generally used for formatting poetry.

2. Right justified -

This style aligns all lines straight with the **right** margin and lets the left margin float with the length of each line as you see I have done with this paragraph.

3. Left justified -

This style aligns all lines straight with the **left** margin and lets the right margin float with the length of each line.

4. Full justification -

This style lays out your page so that both edges are straight up and down an **equal distance** from the edges of the page. It is the style I'm using in writing this book.

The two styles you will want to consider for your book are **Left** and **Full** justification. The best thing for you to do is to simply go to your book shelves and leaf through a few books to observe a few examples of these two styles. **Full** justification is the most popular and looks the best, although left justification can give a more informal letter-type air to it.

2. Footnotes

Footnotes are basically divided into two categories.

1. A simple comment that the author wishes to make without interrupting the narrative of the text.[2]

---

[2] I just put this note here so you could see how it's done. I usually use size 12 for the font in the **text** of my books. But on my **footnotes**, I reduce it to size 10.

Also, although I usually use **full** justification on my text I always use only **left** justification on my footnotes. It serves to give the page a different look. If you really want a different look, you may choose to use

2. A source document that verifies a quotation or reference used in the text. In this case, your footnote should be laid out as follows:

Source author's name, source title [book titles in *italics*, magazine titles underlined], (publishing company: city where the company is located, the year of publication), page number where the quotation is found.

An example:
Gipp, Samuel C., *An Understandable History of the Bible* (DayStar Publishing: Northfield, Ohio, 2000), p.57.

If you should quote the same source **several times in a row**, you need not retype the same information over and over again. Simply type, "Ibid.", and the new page number.

An example:
Ibid., p.83

In the days before computers, the equation by which you figured how much space a footnote took at the bottom of a page was an absolute monster. For that reason, many authors (myself included) replaced "footnotes" with "endnotes." This is where all the source documents were placed at the end of the chapter in which they appeared or, in some cases, at the end of the book. While this was easier on the typesetter, it was more difficult to use for the reader. Today's modern word processing programs all have an easy to use formula for placing footnotes at the bottom of the page where they belong. You should do this so that your book will be a much more useful tool for your reader.

---

a different style font for your footnotes than you use in your text.

3. Type styles

Type styles, or "fonts," come in remarkably diverse styles and designs. Most word processing programs have an extensive fonts library. To this may be added other fonts that you can buy at your local computer or office supply store on a relatively inexpensive CD.

1. The Text - You should use an easily read font for the **text** of your book. **Times New Roman** type is one of the most popular and is extremely easy to read.

Don't use *italics* for the entire text. It may look nice to you, but it is difficult to read. *Italics* and **bold** type may be used for emphasis, though.

2. Chapter titles - Take some quality books and look through them carefully. You will see that they use a different font style for the chapter titles than they do for the text. A type setter uses fonts to lay out a book the same way an artist uses multiple colors to paint a picture. When painting a picture, you don't use just one color or the picture will be boring. You add hints of other colors to brighten it up.

Fonts work the same way. If you use one single font for page headings, chapter titles, and your book's text, it **will** be boring to the eyes. Since books are generally printed only in black and white, you need to use different fonts to work like hints of color to brighten the overall look of the pages of your book. Many an author has presented an excellent argument for his case but bored the eyes of his readers with poor typesetting. **You don't want a boring LOOKING book**

Do not use the "𝔒𝔩𝔡 𝔈𝔫𝔤𝔩𝔦𝔰𝔥" font in your book. 𝔐𝔞𝔫𝔶 𝔞𝔲𝔱𝔥𝔬𝔯𝔰 𝔩𝔦𝔨𝔢 𝔱𝔬 𝔲𝔰𝔢 𝔱𝔥𝔦𝔰 𝔣𝔬𝔫𝔱 𝔟𝔢𝔠𝔞𝔲𝔰𝔢 𝔱𝔥𝔢𝔶 𝔱𝔥𝔦𝔫𝔨 𝔦𝔱 𝔩𝔬𝔬𝔨𝔰 𝔦𝔪𝔭𝔯𝔢𝔰𝔰𝔦𝔳𝔢. 𝔅𝔲𝔱 𝔱𝔥𝔦𝔰 𝔣𝔬𝔫𝔱 𝔦𝔰 𝔬𝔫𝔢 𝔬𝔣 𝔱𝔥𝔢 𝔪𝔬𝔰𝔱 𝔡𝔦𝔣𝔣𝔦𝔠𝔲𝔩𝔱 𝔱𝔬 𝔯𝔢𝔞𝔡 𝔞𝔫𝔡 will ultimately discourage your reader and defeat your purpose for writing the book in the first place. Remember, this is a book, not a work of art.

For this same reason, you **should not** use Roman Numerals for chapter numbers or any other numbering purpose other than the unnumbered opening pages of your book. No one wants to have to try to figure out what all those "I's," "V's," and "X's" mean. You may be thinking that it looks majestic. Your reader will instead be wondering why you intentionally placed unnecessary hurdles in front of him.

4. Widows & Orphans

A widow is the first line of the first paragraph on a page or the last line of the last paragraph on a page that, because of formatting, ends up standing all alone at either the bottom or top of the preceding or following page. An orphan is a single word that does the same. Most word processing programs will have a formula for eliminating this.[3]

5. Page layout

Most books are printed on a standard sized page of 5.5" by 8.5". This will be about the most economical size for your book.

There may be cases where a unique page size is needed. If your book is extremely large you may have to go to a larger page layout so as to reduce the overall thickness of the finished book.

---

[3] I have intentionally not used the programming command to eliminate widows and orphans in this book. Look through its pages and you will come across places where this has occurred.

Please note: You will be sending your printer what is called a "camera ready" manuscript. Most likely this will be on 8.5" x 11" paper. It will be best if your 5.5" x 8.5" text pages are **centered** on these sheets. You can do this easily by setting the **margins** on your page to place your page in the middle of the 8.5" x 11" sheet. To do this, set your margins as follows:

Left - 2.25"
Right - 2.25"
Top - 2"
Bottom - 2"

This setting will place your text in the middle of an 8.5" x 11" page and still give you the optimum space for your text.

When you insert a lengthy quote into the text of your book, there are certain rules to follow. If the quote is three lines long or less, you should treat it as any other part of the text.

If the quote is four lines long or more, it should be indented from the standard page margin. This will keep your reader from "getting lost" and mistaking the quote as your writing.

If your quote runs into more than one paragraph, there is also a rule for quotation marks. You should put quotation marks at the beginning of each paragraph being quoted but **not** at the end until the last paragraph in the quotation. When your readers sees that a paragraph begins with a quotation mark, but has none at the end, it informs them that the quotation is continuing beyond that one paragraph. When they finally arrive at the quotation mark at the end of the final paragraph, they will realize that the quotation is finished.

6. Page headers

Look at any quality book and you will see that it has headers at the top of its pages. Cheap pulp paperbacks will usually have the author's name on the even pages and the book title on the odd pages. Sometimes this arrangement is reversed. There is no right or wrong way to do it.

Page headers can be of an entirely different font than is used anywhere in your book.

People leaf through **magazines** from the back to the front. That's why advertising found on **left pages** costs more than advertising on right ones.

But people leaf through **books** from front to back. Therefore your page headers should be laid out as follows:

Even pages - The even pages will not be seen as easily as the right (or odd-numbered) pages. Therefore ,you should put your book's **title** in the header on the even (or left) pages. Since the person leafing through your book should already know what the name of it is, this is considered the least important of the information you are providing him.

Odd pages - You should place your **chapter titles** on the odd (or right) pages. This will greatly help your readers when they are trying to find something they read earlier. They will see the chapter headers easily.

Since the page header for the even pages will remain the same for every page in the book, most word processing programs will only require that it be inserted into the **first** chapter. As each following chapter is pasted to the end of this one, the header should automatically appear on the newly added chapter.

It is best to make each chapter of your book its own individual computer file while you're writing it. This will help greatly when it is time to add **chapter headers** to the **odd** pages. Insert the chapter header in each individual file designating that you only want it on the odd numbered pages. As each chapter is merged with the one ahead of it when you put the entire book into one file, the chapter header from the preceding chapter will automatically be turned off and the desired one will remain.

The first page of a chapter should have neither a page header nor a page number. Your word processing program should have a command that will **suppress** these functions for the designated pages.

7. Page numbering

You have the option of placing page numbers at the top or bottom of the page. They can be centered (bottom) or held to the outer edge of the page at either the top or bottom of the page.

Your word processing program should have a page-numbering feature that will give you several choices.

As previously mentioned, the easiest way to work on your book on your computer is to make each chapter an individual file. This, of course, will result in each file being at page "1." When you are finished with the text of your book, you will need to activate the page-numbering feature **in chapter one**. Then you will need to select and paste chapter two to the end of chapter one. You will then do the same with each proceeding chapter, selecting and moving it to the end of the one it follows in the book. As this is done, your page numbering feature should automatically number the added pages until you finally have the entire text of your book in one file with the pages numbered properly.

8. Text boxes

Have you ever leafed through a book and noticed that some pages had a quote from the book in larger type, or possibly even a different font? This is a **text box**. These are very useful in type setting. They break up a page that is filled with nothing but text.

Text boxes break up a page that is filled with nothing but text.

Text boxes also give someone leafing thought he book in bookstore a taste of the book to peak their interest. I use them in some of my books but not all. As you can I haven't used them in this book except on this page so you can see how they look.

This is also how you add pictures to your text.

> *You can use a shaded background if you wish.*

Your word processing program should have commands that allow you to insert a text box onto any page you wish. When using text boxes it is best if they pretty much centrally located on the page. Again, the best thing to do is to use a different document and practice making and moving text boxes before you place any in your manuscript.

9. Pages other than text

In all books there are pages that are not part of the text. These occur both at the front and back of the book.

Opening pages - These are obviously the pages you see in the book prior to reaching the text. These pages **are not** included in the numbered pages of your book. They may be numbered with lower case Roman Numerals at the bottom of the pages. I will walk you through these pages as simply as possible. Since your word processing program will automatically start numbering pages from the very first page of a file it may be to your advantage to make the text of your book a separate file from these opening pages. This way you can exclude the page numbering commands from your opening pages while correctly numbering the pages for the text of your book.

1. First sheet - This is the first sheet of paper you will see upon opening the front cover of your book. It should be **totally blank**. Someone, somewhere, is going to ask you to sign their copy of your book. It is far easier to sign a blank page than a page with printing on it such as the Title Page.

2. Title Page - This page follows the first sheet. It has **only** the title of the book with no other information on it. The back of this page should be left blank.

3. Author's Title Page - This page follows the Title Page. It has three forms of information on it: the book title, the author's name, and the name of the publishing company.

4. Copyright Page - This page is actually the back of the Author's Title Page. It will contain your copyright date, ISBN number, and Library of Congress number. It can also include any "1st Printing", "2nd Printing", etc. information you wish and any other information or disclaimers you need to convey to the reader.

5. Books by This Author - If you have written more than one book you may include a page that lists the titles of these works. The back of this page is blank.

6. Dedication - It is not necessary to dedicate your book to anyone. Many authors wax romantic at this point. But there may be a legitimate desire to do so. The back of this page is blank.

7. Table of Contents - This page is self explanatory. It informs your reader where each chapter begins. This can be expanded and thus can be used as a rudimentary index by your reader to help with finding information in your book. (See the Appendix at the back of this book.)

8. Preface - This is a **brief** explanation of your book. A preface **should not** be lengthy. As a rule, the Preface of a book is looked on with disdain by the reader and usually ignored. Therefore, you should try to limit it to one page. It may be an explanation of why you wrote the book. You should begin the numbering of your book's opening pages with Roman Numerals at this page.

9. Introduction - This is to your book what Kindergarten is to school. Not absolutely necessary to be read, yet it should give your reader a head start in understanding your message.

You may have a prominent person write your introduction, but it is not necessary. There seems to be a glamor associated with having a prominent person write the introduction to a book. Of course, there is the increased sense of value that an exotic name adds. But remember, if you haven't put anything worth reading into the book, all the famous people in the world can't make it sell.

Closing Pages - These pages **are** included in the regular page numbering of your book. You may or may not require all of these sections in your book.

1. Appendix - An appendix is information for your reader that is "tacked on" to the back of your book so you don't break up the flow of your narrative. It may be an example of a form you refer to in the text of your book or a detailed list of information for the readers' benefit.

I have placed an appendix in the back of this book for two purposes. First, it is an example of how the table of contents can be laid out for your book. Second, it is an illustration of how to use an appendix so you can determine if your book needs one.

2. Bibliography - This is a list of books, magazines, or other sources you used to write your book. Information in your bibliography is laid out as follows:

Author's Name (last name first), the source title (Book titles in *italics*, magazine titles underlined), the city where it was published, the company that published it, the year it was published.

An example:
Gipp, Samuel C. *Gipp's Understandable History of the Bible*. Miamitown, Ohio: DayStar Publishing, 2000.

3. Index - The index is the last thing you add to your book, but it can be the most important tool you offer your reader. Think. Someone reads your book and later wants to find something that you said. He doesn't remember where it was, but he does remember a key word you used in your explanation. The index should include such key words. Readers can now go to the index, look up the list of places where the word appears in the text, and find the information they are seeking.

Depending on the amount of information your reader may be seeking, you can have several indices. You may have one that refers only to the names of individuals mentioned in your book. You may have one that lists Scripture references quoted in your book. You may then have just a general index of prominent words. Usually just a general index is needed.

There should be an index feature on your word processing program. You will first need to determine what words are required to produce a useable index. These will, most likely, be typed into a separate file and this file will then be run through your word processing program's index feature. It may be wise to make a practice index on another document before you endeavor to do so with your book.

The index is to be added **after your book is completely type set**. Only after your page-numbering is done, your page headers completed, and your fonts all chosen and sized properly are you ready to add your index. Why now? Because every one of the above actions has an effect on where a particular word will appear in the text. Only then will your index page numbers be correct.

Your word processing program should have a feature that will generate the desired index. It may take some practice to get it all down right, so you are advised to index some unimportant file first to learn the unique characteristics of your particular program.

10. Proofreading

Your book **must** be proofread by someone other than yourself. The problem with being your own proofreader is that you **know** what you wanted to say, so you will **always see** exactly what you wanted in the text. An outsider will be able to see mistakes you would naturally overlook.

A proofreader will also pick up problems that your spell checker will overlook. Sometimes you may mistakenly type "form" instead of "from." A spell checker will skip over this error while a proof reader should catch it.

Just about every book has a mistake or two that even managed to slip by a proofreader. Once you've written a few books you will tend to be a little more gracious with these when you find them in the books of others.

Cover design

Front cover

We've all heard the saying, "You can't judge a book by its cover." **But people do!** If your cover looks like it was done by a six-year-old with crayons, your book will not sell. Yes, I know, you have a computer graphics program that is "as good as any professional." No, it isn't. Computer generated covers (yes, even color ones) look like...**computer generated covers**.

Having a cover professionally designed is costly. **That's why** you wanted to use your computer in the first place, so you could do it on the cheap. **LOOK!** If your own book isn't worth a decent financial investment from **you**, then throw it away and go back to dreaming! If **you** don't think your book is worth a financial investment, then what does that tell your prospective reader?

Back cover

The back cover of your book can be left blank or used to give someone perusing a bookstore a little information to interest him in your book. It can also include a brief biographical sketch of you, the author. It can even include your picture if you like to be seen.

Whether the back cover is left blank or not, it **will** be the location for your bar code. The bar code will be furnished by your printer. It will include the general book information, including the price. This means you will have to send the book to the printer, get an estimate of what it will cost to print it and then multiply that by four and tell them the price to put in the bar code. As distasteful as it may seem, it is wise to reduce the price of your book by a penny or two so it will fall beneath the rounded dollar. In other words, price it at $9.95 rather than $10.00. Don't call it dishonest. Wal-Mart does it all the time and you love it!

Spine

The spine of your book should contain three bits of information:

    1. The title of the book
    2. The author's last name
    3. The name or logo of the book's publishing company.

Your cover most likely will be paper, as hard covers

tend to be beyond the financial reach of most people. You will need to have them "film laminated." This is a process that helps them resist scuffing.

Necessary numbers

1. ISBN number

ISBN stand for International Standard Book Numbering. If someone has the ISBN number for your book, he can go to any bookstore, locate it, and buy it.

You can obtain an ISBN number for your book by writing:

ISBN Agency
R. R. Bowker
121 Chanlon Rd.
New Providence, NJ 07974

Or call: 908-665-6770, or FAX 908-665-2895.

The R. R. Bowker Corporation, the caretakers of the ISBN system, will send you either a block of 10 or 100 ISBN numbers, depending on how many books you expect to print. These will be assigned by you to each book and returned to a different address than the one to which you applied to get the numbers. There will be a service charge. Currently that charge is $175.00, although, like everything else, it will go up with time.

2. Library of Congress number

The Library of Congress number is obtained to help

let the Library of Congress know that your book exists. You write and ask for each individual LOC number, and then you are to send them a complimentary book when your book is printed.

You can apply for a Library of Congress number by writing:

>The Library of Congress
>Cataloging in Publication Division
>Washington, D.C.
>20540-4320

Or call: 202-707-6372.

3. Bar code

The bar code is used in many ways by a bookstore. It is entered into their computer upon receipt of a book and then deleted when that book is sold. In this manner the bookstore keeps a running inventory of the books it has in stock.

It is also scanned at the check out counter so the customer can be charged.

Just about all businesses use this method of stock and price recording. If you do not have a bar code on your book, they cannot do this and **will not** be inclined to handle your book. It doesn't matter how important you think your book is or what you think about "the mark of the beast." They simply are not going to go through the trouble of carrying a book that does not fit the system they use.

If you are **convinced** that the bar code is the mark of the beast and using it is satanic, I suggest you **keep** that conviction and stick by it no matter what anybody tells you. Why? Because that means you will **never** have a book published and you are the very type that the public **does not** need to hear from!

Copyright

Most authors do not understand the copyright. The word "copyright" simply means "right to copy." In other words, no one can take a book and copy it without permission from whoever holds the "right to copy" the book. No one "grants" you a copyright for your book. You **automatically own** the "right to copy" **any** books you've written. This "copy right" begins when you finish the book and is your property until fifty years after your death. The only reason you send in for a "copyright" is to let the copyright office know that your book exists.

Think about it: you write a book, and two years later someone begins to reproduce your book under his own name. You want to stop this. You contact the copyright office. Unfortunately, not being clairvoyant, they do not even know that your book exists. Plus, if the pirate author has filed for a copyright of "his" book, you will be headed for a lawsuit since you will no longer be free to copy your own book. After years of court battles and piles of money, you will most likely win this case. But do you really want to fight it in the first place?

The copyright also protects you from having an unscrupulous person alter your book a little and reissue it under **your** name to make it seem that you are saying something that you never intended to say.

The copyright isn't about **money**. It's about

protection.

> You can contact the copyright office at:
> Library of Congress
> Copyright Office
> Washington, D.C.
> 20559

Or call: 202-707-3000.

What about the money?

There are two types of money I refer to here.

1. The money you spend to get your book printed and published.

2. The money you will make from the sale of your book.

1. The expense of printing and publishing your book.

As mentioned in the preface, most wannabe authors think that they are someday going to be "discovered." To this end, they usually send their book, in manuscript form, to publishing companies and prominent people, unsolicited. Their hope is that someone will recognize the intrinsic value of their work and offer to publish it free of charge. With this same vain hope I sent my Master's thesis to countless individuals. Other than Dr. David Otis Fuller asking if he could write the introduction, I got no takers. This is no complaint against those I sent it to. It was sent unsolicited, they had their own lives and ministries to conduct, and even those who may have been favorably impressed (there was one person) are probably not in any position to do anything about it. Add to that the fact that they didn't know me from Adam and it is completely understandable **and** acceptable that they would ignore my contact. Seven years after I first wrote it, I finally printed it myself under the title *An Understandable History of the Bible*. That's really how it should have been.

I have for years received those same type of unsolicited manuscripts. Since I am **buried** in trying to fulfill my own calling and usually working on about four books myself, I am unable to help even if I am impressed to. Therefore, they usually go unread or unpublished. (There was just **one** manuscript which was so impressive that I called its author and told him he was doing Christianity an injustice if he didn't get it published. He did so and Bible-believing Christianity has been served by that book in a way that no other could have.)

It is not all selfishness that initiates such contacts. There are two very valid reasons why people hope that someone else will take the burden of publishing their book off their hands.

1. People have a total void of knowledge in knowing what to do to get a book into **print**, let alone **published**. They don't know about copyrights, ISBN numbers, Library of Congress numbers, and other incidentals that their book needs. Beyond that, they have no concept of how to make contacts that will put their book on bookstore shelves (publishing), where it can be discovered and purchased.

These people simply see someone else as an answer to all these problems. They think, "I'll send my book to so-in-so and he'll like it, see the critical need to get it printed, and take care of it for me." There is no greed, pride, or laziness involved here. It is just a vain hope that all of the things they lack will be provided voluntarily by someone else. Part of this is due to their total ignorance of the effort required to see a finished manuscript come into print. They mistakenly think that the most difficult part of publishing a book is **the writing** of it. I have often told people that after I write the final word into a book, the effort required to convert it into a printed and bound volume that I can hold in my hand is **greater** than that which was required to write it. You don't believe that? Then explain why there are countless **unpublished** books in manuscript form. It's because **writing** is the easy part! Who wouldn't like to simply sit around and write all day long and then deliver a finished manuscript to someone else, who returned several days later with a finished book? (Quit thinking about Tom Clancy! You're **not** Tom Clancy!)

  2. The second reason young authors hope someone will publish their book for them is monetary. They don't think they have enough money to see their book through to print, so they hope someone else, **with enough money**, will be favorably impressed and do it for them.[4]

  Along with this is the added fact that they don't want to gamble with their **own** money. You see, they think that they have written a guaranteed best-seller. Thus, they are doing the company they send their manuscript to **a favor** by allowing them to handle the book for them. They are sure that

---

[4] The fact is that they **may** have enough money but simply overestimate the cost or volume of their printing.

there is no "gamble" involved. But when the thought turns to investing their **own** money, they feel a little differently. They **still** have no doubt that their book will sell in the millions of copies. But they fear they may not be able to make the connections necessary for its success. Suddenly they have better things to do with their money. So they send their manuscript off to someone who they hope will have no such reservations about investing in their "sure thing."

Again, I have no condemnation for these people. We **all** have been in the same place with the same fears and feelings. Unfortunately, it simply is not a **realistic** point of view and the sooner it is discarded, the sooner you can move in the direction of making progress. As I've already said, if **you** aren't willing to invest some money into your book, why do you think someone else should?

2. The money you will make from the sale of your book.

The money you make from the sale of your book is called "profit." You already knew that, but I needed to put the word in print where you had to face it. Amazingly, people who think that there is nothing wrong with making a profit in other areas become good **communists** when they discuss the profit from the sale of books. Especially **somebody else's** books! At this point, in a desperate and futile effort to look spiritual, readers and authors alike allow their human nature to take over and the result is both ridiculous and destructive.

It sounds so pious to Christians for an author to say, "I make no profit from my books." What he is trying to say is, "Please don't hate me or think I'm greedy. No, I'm a good communist and would never be so **carnal** as to even consider making **money** off of you." Of course, any **thinking** person knows that money can somehow find it's way into the author's pocket without being labeled as "profit" just as surely as a preacher can get money that isn't taxed because he found a way not to have to list it as "income." **Get real!**

A question I have often asked a person who thinks it is sinful to sell a book and profit from their labor is, "If you paint a house, do you think it's all right to get paid and realize a profit for **that** labor?"

"Of course."

"Then why is it wrong for people who write a book to profit from **their** labor?"

The **fact** is that there is no **scriptural** reason why it is wrong to make a profit from the work involved in writing and publishing a book. Attacking that profit is just a cheap way for very small people to attempt to look spiritual. I have even heard of some authors (who are "proud of their humility") very piously state, "**My** books are **free** because **I** don't believe it is right to make a profit on selling books." What they **actually** mean is that they doubt anyone would ever pay even a dollar for their books, so they have to **give** them away. Then they seek to hide this fear by sounding spiritual. If unspiritual people, trying to pass themselves off as spiritual, were still dealt with like they were in Acts 5, there would be few phonies boasting about how godly they are!

The **fact** is that according to the **Bible**, it **isn't** wrong, sinful, or immoral to profit from one's labor, as is pointed out clearly in Ecclesiastes 3:13, "And also that every man should eat and drink, and enjoy the good of all his labour, it is the gift of God." Now, are **you** going to place yourself above the Bible and deny someone the enjoyment of the fruit of his labor? Are

you going to deny him "the gift of God?"

This ridiculous situation arises because of envy. We Americans have made the statement "All men are created equal" into a Bible doctrine. Thus, if someone has the ability to write and publish a book, **it can't be** because he is smarter than we are. Then we wouldn't be equal. So it must be because he has access to some help that we don't have. Therefore, it would be unfair **and unspiritual** if he profits from such an unfair advantage.

Grow up! There are people who possess artistic and musical talent that I will **never** have. That isn't unfair, it's a fact of life. Am I supposed to cry "Foul!" if they profit from this? There are people who have what it takes to print and publish a book and actually have that book become a profitable seller. There are others who couldn't profitably author a coloring book. Is that unfair? No. Is it something to be ashamed of? Of course not. You find what you can do in this life and do it.

You can plainly see the trials of painting a one hundred and fifty foot high water tower, so you do not begrudge the painter the profit he earns for his effort. If you knew the effort that went into writing, printing, and publishing a book, (it **is** a little tougher than operating a TV remote control), you might learn to be a bit more reasonable and charitable.

If you write a book and make money from it, you have every right in the world to spend every dime on a roomful of Snickers candy bars if you so desire. It's **your** money and the lame "conviction" of some do-nothing Christian shouldn't matter in the least.

With that point made, I am now going to contradict

it. Although I do not believe it is morally wrong to spend the money you realize from the sale of a book on yourself, I think it is financially unsound.

  I am an evangelist. My family and I live on the road fifty-two weeks a year. We have no guaranteed income from anywhere. To live, we have two sources of income. We **live** off of only whatever a church chooses to collect during a meeting. It's called a "love offering." From these offerings we buy our food, clothing, and gasoline and pay for other living expenses. But I never use any of this money to print books. I **print books** only off of what they generate themselves through sales. We have lived by a simple policy for years: **Never** use "love offering" money to print books. If the books can't take care of themselves, then I'll quit writing. **Never** use book money to live off of. If I can't make it on love offerings, I'll get off the road.

  This is a simple principle but it works.[5] The first book I wrote was *An Understandable History of the Bible*. I had just one thousand books printed. The sale of these books provided the capital for printing my second book, *The Answer Book*. The sale of this book provided money to print the second printing of *An Understandable History of the Bible*. The sale of this book provided for the printing of my next book and so on down the line. Although I had the right to spend the money from any of these printings on anything I wanted to, if I had done so I would have had no way to pay

---

[5] The "fly" in this ointment is the countless books I give away to preachers, missionaries, and anyone else I think a book will help. This isn't sound fiscal policy, but I figure I wrote them to be a help rather than to become a millionaire, so that's just the way it goes!

for the printing of the next one. Thus, although I believe the money is mine to do with as I please, I further think that my books should be financed by and of themselves or they won't get printed.

At this point some Christian con-man is going to say, "Well, I believe that God's people should pay for all the work I'm doing for them so they should provide the funds to print my books." No, you don't. You're just a shyster who is looking for some way to con God's people into supporting you. You, like many, think that people **owe** you something for what you do. You're a **bum**! You're a crook! You take financial advantage of the goodness of God's people. If you were here right now, I would kick you!

Yes, people **do** owe you something for what you've done in writing a book, **and they pay it when they buy the book!** That's why books shouldn't be free.

Have I ever had anyone give me money to help print a book? Yes, of course. But it is a dangerous thing because you can learn how to play on people's hearts to get money out of them. What I would like is for someone to pay to print **all** of my books and let me sit back and do nothing but write and cash checks. But that is the attitude of my wicked human heart. If you don't curb it, you will take unfair advantage of well-meaning people. The **very** people you claim you want to help. Remember, they owe us **nothing** but the price of a book. Don't get proud and see yourself through glasses that no one else is wearing.

In dispensing your books, you should neither play the piety game of charging nothing nor the con-man game of begging funds. Stand on your own two feet! Pay for the first printing out of your own pocket. Pay for the succeeding printings out of what you make from the sale of the books already printed. What? Did you say, "I tried that and it didn't work."? Then maybe God is trying to tell you that your books aren't as needed as you think they are. Go paint a house!

2
What's the Difference Between "printing" and "publishing"?

What's the Difference?

Most people do not understand the difference between the printing and the publication of a book. This misconception exists because the standard perception people have about writing a book is that you write a book, send it to some mystical company somewhere, and it prints the book, places it in bookstores all over the country, and sends you checks to cash the rest of your life.

Printing

When you finish writing your book, you will have it in **manuscript form.** You then have this manuscript printed and bound into a volume. What you now hold in your hand is your book in **printed form.**

Publishing

Publishing is the vehicle by which the public in general discovers that your book exists. You can print 5,000 copies of your book, but people won't buy it if they don't know it exists. Publishing is "proclaiming" the existence of your book so that the public at large can benefit from your great wisdom.

What you need to get a book PRINTED

You need a computer

You can handwrite all the manuscripts in the world, but your book is still going to be typed into a computer at some point, so you may as well start there. Choose a word processing program you like. (Word and WordPerfect are the most popular.)

You need a laser printer

It doesn't matter how good you claim your bubble jet is, it doesn't compare to a laser printer. After seeing the product of a bubble jet next to that of a laser printer, you will understand. Laser printers used to be expensive but can now be purchased for about what a good color bubble jet costs.

If you simply cannot afford a laser printer, then you can take your book, on disk, to a quick-print shop and have it produce a laser printed copy for you.

What's a "book" and what's a "booklet"?

It will be easier to define what a book is by first defining what a booklet is.

What is a booklet?

A booklet is defined by how it is bound. It is usually of few enough pages that it is simply 8.5" x 11" paper folded in half and **saddle stapled**. Many times this can be done "in house" without a professional printer. Pages can be formatted on a computer and then copied on a copier and stapled together along with the cover. If there are few enough pages, there will even be no need to trim the edges although this does give the finished work a very unprofessional, and consequently unattractive, look.

What is a book?

A book is a larger work than a booklet and requires professional binding. This may incorporate a paper cover stock and glue binding or a hard cover binding. The hard cover binding is the more expensive of the two bindings.

If the book is glue-bound, following the binding process, it will need to be trimmed on three sides to make sure the edges of all the pages are even.

For most authors, especially new ones, the cost of producing multiple copies of their book is a major factor. Thus, the most cost effective, **quality** product comes from glue binding. This is also known as "perfect" binding.

Steps to the Printer

1. Finished draft

The finished draft of your book is what you have after you have typed your final word of text. You should run this through your spell checker and correct any other imperfections that you find in the text at this time.

2. Proofreading

After you have given your draft a final going over, you should send it to your proofreader. As stated earlier, **do not** attempt to proofread your own work. You will always overlook errors that an objective reader will catch.

You should actually have **two** separate manuscripts for your book at this time. You should have a larger manuscript which is the **text** of your book and a smaller manuscript which will contain the "Opening Pages" referred to in the previous chapter. This smaller manuscript will probably not need to be sent to your proofreader.

3. Formatting

Once your draft is returned from the proofreader, it is time to format it. When you are finished with this step, you should have a picture on your computer screen of exactly what each printed page should look like.

1. Page size - It is at this time that you will resize your book's page to the size you desire for the finished product.

2. Headers - Now is the time to add the headers at the top of the pages.

3. Page numbering - This is also when you add the page numbers to your book.

4. Fonts styles and sizes - This is the time when you will decide which particular fonts you wish to use for text, headers, title page, chapter titles, and in-text headings, as well as pick any other special fonts needed in the production of your book.

5. Page layout - During the formatting of your book,

you will need to eliminate "widows and orphans." Most word processing programs have a "Keep it Together" command that, once enabled, will automatically perform this function for you.

Also, you may need to manually move a heading to a following page during this step so that it does not appear disconnected from the subject it introduces.

6. Chapter title pages - Some authors like to have all of the chapters in their book begin on a right-handed page. If you desire this, you may need to enable an "Add a Page" command at the end of a chapter in order to move the next chapter title page back to a right-handed page.

7. Opening pages - **Once you finish** formatting the text of your book, it is time to do the opening pages. This is done **after** the text because you cannot insert the correct page numbers into your table of contents and indices until you have finished formatting the text.

8. Index - Now that you have finalized the page numbers in your book, you can run the index feature in your word processing program. You will want to add the index to the end of the text of your book so that it's pages are correctly numbered.

Inserting an index should be **the very last** thing you do before printing your manuscript from a laser printer in preparation to send to your printer. It must be done only when you are certain **you will not add another word** to the text. If you insert your index and then make changes to your text the words your index includes may not be found on the page that your index says they will due to the change in page alignment from the added words.

4. Cover

By this time you should have had the cover art

finished for your book. It may be best to have your graphics man contact your printer directly so that they can determine what the printer needs from him. He may be able to send a disk rather than a hard copy to the printer.

Your graphics man will need a page count of your book so that he knows how thick the spine will be.

Once you have completed all of the above steps, you are ready to send your laser-printed manuscript to the printer. This is known as a "perfect" manuscript. It is also called "camera ready."

At the Printer

Kill the Dream!

Before you send your manuscript to a printer, it is presumed that you have checked with several for the best price. Now the question is this: "How many books should I have printed?"

Before you determine how many copies you will have printed, you will need to deal with "Gold Fever." We have all heard of men who claimed land on which they hoped to find gold. Many of these men had **visions** of striking it rich. They saw themselves both rich and famous. They envisioned themselves as soon needing never to work again.

Believe it or not, you will experience a similar condition prior to printing your first book. You will have visions of it becoming a best-seller. You will see fame and fortune "forced" upon you. You may foresee that you will have to "quit your day job" in order to meet the demand for further works. (You **may** wake up now!)

This fantasy is neither sinful nor selfish. It is simply **natural** and undoubtedly **inaccurate**. You will need to deal with this fictional vision and hold it in check before you order the printing of your book, or else you will have an unreasonable number of books printed and find yourself stuck with them when they don't become as popular in **real life** as they were in your dream.

How many books should I have printed?

Because of the advent of pulp fiction, the immense fame of the authors of such works, and the *New York Times* best-seller list, first-time authors tremendously overestimate the number of books they should print. They simply cannot help but envision the selling of **millions** of books. Of course, in an effort to be realistic, they only intend to print about 30,000 books during their first printing. This is a wonderful way to destroy yourself financially.

Because of the popularity of "million-sellers," few people realize that if a book sells a mere **5,000 copies,** it has done well. That's right. Five thousand copies. I know, I know. But **your** book is going to be "discovered" and find itself on the shelves of major bookstores, which will insure sales figures in the hundreds of thousands, at least. Like I said, **"Kill the dream!"**

What did you think just now? "But if I only sell 5,000 books, I'll **never** end up rich!" I thought you were writing because you had something someone needed and just wanted to get the material into the hands of those whom it would help? What? How can you **really** help people with such a small printing? It's called **reality**. You are a fool to assume the sale of a large number of books.

But it gets worse!

You see, you shouldn't plan on printing even 5,000 books. Do you know 5,000 people? Why do you think 5,000 total strangers are going to pick up your book and feel an irresistible need to buy it? Why do you think that a bookstore, which has as its first goal that of turning a profit, is going to look at **your** book and see a financial goldmine? **"Kill the dream!"**

Using your head

For the first printing of your first book, I would recommend no fewer than **200** and **no more** than **500** books. That's right; I didn't forget to put a zero on the end of that figure. I said, "500," not "5,000."

There are two simple reasons for printing such a small number of books the first time around.

1. Money

Unless you are independently wealthy, you are not going to have a great deal of cash with which to print your book. I do not recommend borrowing money from friends or financial institutions in order to print your book. This means you will have to print it with "cash-on-hand." Most people do not have the finances needed to print 5,000 books. Such a printing could run in the tens of thousands of dollars.

Furthermore, I **do not** recommend using your retirement or investment money on printing your book, even though you may be convinced that it's a "sure thing" that the book will sell. Instead of having visions of **success,** you need to entertain a vision of **failure.** Think for a moment that your book absolutely **flops** and sells about 25 copies. Would you rather have **475** books left rotting in your garage or **4975**? Would you rather have to write off as **lost** the cost of **500** books or **5,000**?

2. Realistic sales estimates

As I have already mentioned, you **must** consider the chance that your book is **not** going to sell. If you refuse to even consider such a negative response to your book, you are living in a dream world and will soon find yourself broke (at best) and in great debt (at worst).

Remember, after printing your book you will need a place to store your printed books. Let us assume that there will be 50 books per box after printing. Two hundred books will amount to only four boxes. Not a very difficult storage problem. Five hundred books will equal ten boxes. A little more difficult than four but not impossible. Now try storing **one hundred** boxes of books (5,000 books total). You can see that the problem can get out of hand quickly.

What? You thought that this big publishing company was going to handle your books and **it** would take on the responsibility of how many books are printed and where they are stored? Fine. Put this book down and go get the contract! When you have exhausted your efforts and hopes, come back to this place in the book and we'll talk. I'm certain you'll be more ready to listen then.

Again, I **strongly** recommend the printing of no more than 500 books your first time out. You may ask, "But what if the book becomes popular and sells out quickly and then I have no stock to meet the demand?"

Point #1: It's **not** going to sell out that quickly.

Point #2: If you carefully monitor the rate at which the first printing sells, you should be able to estimate the needed size of the second printing. At that time you will have three options:

1. Reprint the book at the **same number** as the first printing.

2. Increase the number of books printed. Maybe do 700 or even 1,000 this time.

3. If I'm wrong and your book is swept from bookstore shelves in a matter of days, you may print several thousand books in your second printing. I still would not advise more than 5,000 copies and then **only** if you have the cash-in-hand to do it.

How much should you charge per book?

As mentioned earlier, most people who give their books away realize that few people would pay money for them. Thus they give them away. But, ever quick to turn a **necessity** into a **virtue,** they piously proclaim that they "refuse" to take money for their books. Think about it. Even **toilet paper** has a sales value. Are you printing something that you claim has less value than toilet paper?

Establishing the retail price for a book **is not** an arbitrary act where you sit down and say, "I think **that** will be enough to charge." There is an equation that has been long used by publishers to determine the retail price of a book. This equation was revealed to me many years ago by a book

What's the Difference Between "printing" and "publishing"?

retailer, and it has within it enough of a profit margin to cover hidden costs that you may overlook or underestimate if you simply "ballpark" a figure that sounds good to you.

To establish the proper, "safest," retail price for your book, you should take the **individual** cost of printing one book and multiply it times **five**.

Example: If your book costs you $2.00 per copy to have printed, you should affix a retail price of $10.00 to it. Again, immediately there will either be cries of "rip-off!" or false dreams of making millions of dollars selling your book. Neither is true.

It doesn't take a genius to see that one hundred books printed at $2.00 apiece will cost $200 to print and then sell for $1,000, returning a healthy profit of $800. The math is right; it's the assumption that's wrong. You may say, "Why can't I just add one dollar to the price I paid? Then I can sell the book for $3.00. It will be more affordable and I still make a profit." The answer is simple. If you print a book for $2.00 and sell it for $10.00 you will **never** make $8.00 profit per book. It simply will not happen.

The misconception of $800 profit comes from not including **unseen** costs involved in the printing and marketing of a book. It is so **natural** to overlook these costs that wiser minds than yours and mine established the 1 x 5 equation long before you and I were born.

Hidden costs

There are so many costs to marketing a book, that even though I will attempt to include them all, you will probably find there are some that I fail to mention.

1. Shipping - Although the shipping costs of filling

individual orders for your book will be paid by the purchaser, there will be the **initial shipping** cost of having the finished books shipped to your home or place of storage.

 2. Storage - You may be able to store all of your books in your home or garage. But remember, after your book begins to sell by the thousands and people are clamoring for it, you will have to print it in larger numbers, which may require a dedicated storage area.

 3. Advertising - You may be marketing a certain amount of your books yourself and may desire to place ads for it in related publications. You are about to find out how expensive paid advertisements are!

 4. Give-aways - Although you intend to sell your books, you will be surprised at the great number that you will simply give away. You will give free copies to your family and your friends. Then you may pass on copies to people you meet with an interest in the subject you wrote about.[6]

 If you try to place your book in a bookstore, you will end up giving a free copy to the store manager for approval. These are called "promotional gifts" and are tax-deductible.

 The greatest number of give-aways will be "worthy causes." I give hundreds of books away. In fact, I give away so many that it hurts my ability to print new books at times. I'm a sucker in this manner, but I do not see myself changing much before the Rapture. I have sent **hundreds** of free books to missionaries upon request. I once sent $500 worth of books to China, free. In addition to the free books, it cost me $250

---

[6] As an example, this book itself will probably be given away free to countless would-be authors whom I simply want to help.

What's the Difference Between "printing" and "publishing"?

just to ship them. Do I regret it? Of course not. But I am awfully thankful for whoever figured out the 1 x 5 pricing equation.

5. Discounts - If you could actually sell 100 books which cost you $200 to print for $1,000 dollars, you would **theoretically** make $800. (Remember: your books should pay for themselves. Thus, by banking your entire income from the books, you will have money to pay for the next printing.)

The fact is that you will **never** sell a great number of books if you intend on selling them all yourself. (Do you think Tom Clancy became a million-selling author by hawking his books on some street corner?) You will need to get your book onto bookstore shelves. Well, do you think that a **bookstore** is going to pay you $10.00 per book and then turn around and sell it for $10.00? Of course not. It is going to expect you to sell your book to it at a discounted price. Again, this price will not be what you arbitrarily decide. There are certain discount prices that have already been established. You may say that you refuse to accept them. Fine. Retailers will simply refuse to sell your book. Their shelves are already full of books which they bought at their discount. They don't need yours.

1. Bookstore discounts - Bookstores will expect to buy your book at a **40%** discount off the retail price. That means you will be selling it to a bookstore for only **$6.00** rather than $10.00.

Remember: although many small bookstores like to refer to themselves as a "ministry," they **need** to make a certain amount of money to stay open. They have rent, payroll, health insurance, Social Security payments, advertising of their own, and innumerable unseen costs.

Don't begrudge them a profit. They **need** a profit as much as want a profit. They cannot stay open if they pay more than 60% of retail price for the books they stock. But if you manage to sell your book to every bookstore in your locality, you will still be greatly limited in the size of the market you will reach. You need to sell your book to the folks who sell to the bookstores!

2. Distributor discounts - As a rule, bookstores do not buy their stock directly from an author. They buy them from a book distributor. One book distributor may supply books to a multitude of bookstores. If you get your book into **one** bookstore, that is good; but if you can get your book accepted by a **distributor,** then you will have automatic access to a great number of individual bookstores, thus multiplying your opportunity to sell books.

Now, try **thinking** again. If a mere **bookstore** has a good deal of overhead costs, then a distributor, which is much larger, is going to have **much greater** overhead costs. Think again. If the distributor buys books from you for 60% of the retail cost, then it has to turn around and sell those books to a bookstore at the same price. It simply won't work. It will go broke and the system collapses.

For this reason, if you are able to get a distributor to handle your books, it will expect a **60%** discount. This allows it to sell your book to a bookstore and make 20% profit. Notice that you are now down to making a mere $2.00 per book rather than the imaginary $8.00. Yet you still may make more money this way since your chance of selling more books increases when selling through a distributor. Thus, you make your profit on volume. In other words, would you rather sell **one book** yourself at an $8.00

profit or **ten books** through a **bookstore** for a total of $40.00 profit or **fifty books** through a **distributer** at a total $100 profit? Do the math! Also, if you really do simply desire to "just get the information out" rather than realize wealth, you can see that the system still works to your advantage by getting more books out than you can singlehandedly.

Following are the pros and cons of the system:
Selling books individually:
    Pro - You make 80% profit.
    Con - You have only the limited market of people you come into contact with personally.
Selling books through a bookstore:
    Pro - A bookstore has a greater area market in which to sell books than individuals.
    Con - You make only a 40% profit per book.
Selling books to a distributor:
    Pro - You will greatly increase the chance of selling your book since it will now have access to numerous bookstores and their larger markets.
    Con - You will make only a 20% profit per book.

I need to remind you that the success of your book, though greatly enhanced by wider distribution, will **actually** be decided on how well the public at large accepts what you are offering them. If they don't buy it, then **no one** can magically make it sell.

Part Two:

DayStar Publishing: A New Concept in Publishing

3
What DayStar Publishing IS

The Need for DayStar

As mentioned earlier, **publishing** a book is the method used to let the public at large know that your book exists and is available for purchase. Publishing a book is actually far more difficult than **printing** one. Although you can print countless books, people won't buy them if they don't know they exist.[7]

There have always been two methods for publishing a book. One, go all over the country at your own expense and visit bookstore after bookstore and try to get them to sell your book, or two, sell your book (in manuscript form) to a large publishing company that will print and publish the book at its own expense.

---

[7] I know of a man who wrote a worthy book. He then printed 5,000 copies. That was years ago and the vast majority of those books are rotting in his garage unsold. Why? No one knows it exists! It's been **printed** but not **published**.

It is obvious that the second option is the most attractive as well as most practical. All you need to do is write the books and the publishing company does the rest. Unfortunately, it is also the most difficult to achieve.

DayStar Publishing falls between these two options. It is bigger and more efficient than marketing your book individually, yet small enough to be accessible to more individuals.

An idea is born

The idea for DayStar Publishing came to me while I was recuperating from a recent surgery. The surgery had alleviated a great deal of pain that I had been experiencing. The elimination of this pain allowed that portion of my brain which had been forced to try to suppress the pain to be free to be used for plain old **thinking**.

I had been burdened for quite a while that books written by King James Bible believers were ending up on the shelves of other King James Bible believers and nowhere else. Although this might allow for the selling of many books, it didn't accomplish these authors' primary desire. This desire is to get their material into the hands of **non**-Bible believers so that they can understand the correctness of the pro-King James position. To do this, it would be necessary to place the books of Bible-believing authors onto the shelves of mainstream Christian bookstores, where they at least had a chance of being "discovered" by the general public.

But there were several major obstacles to placing the books of Bible-believing authors on the shelves of mainstream bookstores. Although there are quite a few Bible-believing authors who have much to offer on the subject, they are **all** basically their own publishing company. As a rule, bookstores do not buy their stock from individual authors. This effectively locked Bible-believing authors out of mainstream bookstores.

Mainstream bookstores buy their stock from publishing companies. We all know the name of one or two of these. But these companies are not interested in publishing books supporting the King James position. Thus, no Bible-believing authors has ever had their books accepted by a major publishing company.[8] Every King James Bible-believing author is basically a "one man show."

The problem was obvious. How could Bible believers get their books into the catalog of a publishing company so that they as least had a chance of having their books reach the shelf of a mainstream bookstore?

With brain power that was now freed up to **think**, I began to ponder the problem. The answer came so quickly and was so simple that I was embarrassed that I hadn't thought of it before (although I knew **why** I hadn't thought of it before).

I decided to found a publishing company that would

---

[8] I know of only one exception to this. Dr. David Otis Fuller had three different pro-King James titles published by Kregel in Grand Rapids, Michigan. But that is as far as it went. In 1980 Dr. Fuller took my master's thesis to Kregel and tried to get the company to publish it. The publisher refused. It told him that it published **his** books because they made the publisher money, but it was not interested in publishing books that concerned the King James issue. It was seven years before I was able to print the volume myself under the title *An Understandable History of the Bible*.

be available to Bible believers. We could pool all our titles under one company name. The company would produce a catalog of books it offered so that bookstores could see if there was anything they wished to offer to their customers. It would not guarantee success, but at least it may grant us **access** to an area that needs to read what Bible believers have to say.

What IS DayStar?

DayStar Publishing is a **publishing company**. But that definition must be explained so there can be no confusion.

1. DayStar is a company

When most people hear the word "company," they envision huge buildings with corporate offices filled with secretaries and executives bustling about making multi-million dollar decisions. Well, you can forget that. That is not the definition of "company" that DayStar subscribes to. In actuality, DayStar Publishing Company is just what it says it is. It is a "company" of like-minded men and women who are joined together to accomplish a single purpose. There are no corporate office buildings and million dollar CEO's. DayStar is **me**! It is me and **you** and **anyone** who wishes to add his efforts and influence to further the cause of God's perfect Bible. Most certainly it will not be a company that agrees together in all of our convictions and interpretations of Scripture. We are not that idealistic. If you demand agreement with your every point of interpretation, you need to look elsewhere. DayStar is not for you. If you can't find the

What DayStar Publishing IS

grace within yourself to work together with others toward a cause that is bigger than you, then you just need to go mow your grass. It's probably **the only thing** you can do without arguing with someone.

2. DayStar is a publishing company

DayStar is a **publishing** company, not a **printing** company. Few people realize that many publishing companies do not have printing capabilities. That is what DayStar is. We will not take books in manuscript form and **print** them. We will take books that are printed by the author and **publish** them. We will offer them a place in our catalog and make them available to mainstream bookstores so that those authors have a chance at having their ideas disseminated among the public at large. We cannot guarantee acceptance. We cannot guarantee sales. (No one can.) We can only place our catalog in the hands of as many mainstream bookstore managers as possible and let the issue develop from there. We promise little more than that.

Obviously, the more individual authors that DayStar can offer to bookstores, the more chance we have of being accepted as a whole.

Legitimate offerings

DayStar has no intention of deceiving anyone: not authors, not bookstore managers. The King James movement is **huge**. You cannot have such a large group of people without having a great deal of talent lying dormant. Bible teaching, history, poetry, Sunday School material, fiction, and many other subjects are not being addressed in an effective manner by King James Bible believers. I constantly come across books and booklets written by Bible-believing authors who have something to offer but have no hope whatsoever of reaching their full potential because they are doomed by their "one-man-show" concept. This means they will never have a chance of putting it into the hands of the general Christian public. These people may wish to join DayStar. If they do, mainstream bookstores that carry their works will make the wisdom of these Bible-believing individuals available to their consumers. **All** involved will benefit; the customer, the bookstore, the author...and **the Lord.**

4
What DayStar Publishing ISN'T

DayStar Publishing ISN'T Buildings

DayStar Publishing is not offices, printing presses, and warehouses. Like many publishing companies we have no printing facilities. We do not print books; we publish books. We do not stock huge volumes of books but simply purchase from our authors what is needed to fulfill the demand we receive from the bookstores we service.

DayStar Publishing ISN'T a Bank

The books of our approved authors are printed by whatever means they contract at their expense. We do not supply funds for the printing of any book no matter how promising its chance of sales is.

Many hopeful young authors seek to evade the financial responsibility for the printing of their book. They also desire some sort of insurance against the financial loss that may occur if no one buys their book. This is a wonderful dream but cannot be a reality in a free market system. Neither DayStar nor any other publishing company can afford to finance the dreams of a would-be author at the expense of someone with a legitimate offering.

DayStar Publishing ISN'T a Guarantor of sales

DayStar believes a book is just like a person; it must stand on its own merit. If it has nothing to offer its readers, it will flag in sales and naturally disappear from public view. I know it hurts to think that something you put your time, effort, and heart into might be seen by the general public as having no value, but that is simply a hard fact of life.

If your book has some virtue to offer its readers, it will grow in popularity and sustain its sales just as naturally.

DayStar's part in this equation is to make the Christian public at large aware of the existence of your book. Imagine for a moment that you have two friends, both of outstanding character, who happen to have never met one another. You take it upon yourself to introduce these two individuals to each other. They hit it off and soon become fast friends. That is the part DayStar Publishing plays in the life of your book. We introduce your book to bookstores, individuals, and other prospective "friends." At that point it is up to the character of the book to establish itself.

DayStar Publishing ISN'T a Conglomerate

DayStar Publishing has no desire to curtail the sales

of the books of its approved authors. It does not seek to control copyrights, content, or the printing of your book.

The copyright for your book will remain your exclusive property unless some special arrangement is seen as beneficial to its sales.

Although DayStar may suggest ways in which to make your book more attractive to the public at large, it cannot force you to write (or **not** write) anything. What it **can** do is refuse to be the publisher for your book if it does not feel it wants the book associated with DayStar Publishing.

DayStar Publishing will not print your book, pay to print your book, nor purchase the entire printing of your book. If **you** do not deem **your own** book as worthy of a financial investment of your own money, you cannot expect others to see it as having any value beyond what you have applied to it by your example.

DayStar Publishing ISN'T Disconnected

DayStar Publishing is not a faceless, emotionless corporation. We are people of like passion. We are joined together to further the cause of Christ. Our primary reason for uniting our talents and efforts is to get the materials of King James Bible-believing authors into the hands of the general Christian public, where they have a chance of benefitting from them. Our primary goal isn't even to see to it that anyone makes money, but to see to it that worthy material has a chance of influencing our country to the overall benefit of all concerned.

DayStar Publishing ISN'T Greedy

Many publishing companies put their own profit making their primary goal. This **is not** always due to greed. As a corporation grows larger and, over the course of time, has to acquire more physical holdings, it also **requires** a larger personal income to keep running. It is not even impossible that at some point in the future DayStar Publishing may see a need to acquire holdings that will assist its efforts to distribute the writings of Bible believers.

DayStar Publishing ISN'T for Everyone

You need to read this entire book and then weigh the advantages and disadvantages of having DayStar Publishing publish your book. If you feel you have a better avenue of distribution, then you should pursue that avenue. If you feel that DayStar can be advantageous to the publishing of your book, then you should sign on and join up. Together we'll do all we can to influence our country for Christ.

Part Three:

What can DayStar Publishing do for You?

5
Assistance with Printing

How DayStar can help

DayStar Publishing is a **publishing** company, not a **printing** company. We will not take your book in manuscript form and transform it into a finished book. That is up to you.

DayStar will place the titles of approved books into its catalog and then seek to place that catalog into as many mainstream bookstores as possible. Such approval will have to be secured **before** the book is printed. If you choose to have DayStar publish your printed book, there are several things we will assist you with. All of these functions will need to be taken care of **before** you have your book printed.

1. Contacts

DayStar Publishing will make available to approved authors a limited list of proofreaders, typesetters, graphic artists, and printers who may be able to help you in the needed areas if you do not have anyone to perform these functions for you.

DayStar **will not** perform these tasks for you, but will help you contact someone who may assist you in these important areas.

Assistance with Printing

2. The DayStar logo

If your book is approved for publishing by DayStar, you will receive permission to use the "DayStar Publishing" logo on the author's title page of your book. This logo is **exclusive property** of DayStar Publishing. If you have written numerous books, the DayStar logo may be used **only** on those which we have **approved** for publication. You will have no authority or permission to apply it to any other works, written or otherwise, which you have not received **written** permission from DayStar Publishing to use it on.

This logo **must** be affixed to the author's title page **before** your book is printed.

3. ISBN number

DayStar Publishing will issue you an ISBN number for your approved book. This number will be exclusive to your book and will help bookstores in ordering your book if interested. This will eliminate the need and cost of you securing an ISBN number on your own.

You are also free to contact R. R. Bowker Inc. and secure an ISBN number on your own.

This number **must** be affixed to the copyright page of your book **before** it is printed.

4. Library of Congress number

DayStar Publishing will submit the necessary forms to the Library of Congress and secure a Library of Congress number for your book.

You are also free to contact the Library of Congress and secure a Library of Congress number on your own.

This number **must** be affixed to the copyright page of

your book **before** it is printed.

What about the copyright?

As explained in Part 1, Chapter 1, you **automatically** control the copyright for any book you write. It begins the moment you finish the book and is your exclusive property until it expires fifty years after your death. A copyright may be sold or given away. It is **never** granted by the government. It is **recognized** by the government. The government requests that you contact it concerning your book only so it is made aware of the existence of your book.

Your copyright is more for protection than an assurance of endless wealth.

DayStar Publishing's desire is to **help** authors, not **control** them. Furthermore, we will not be printing your book, so there is no need for you to give up your copyright. It will remain your exclusive property.

There may be some special case where a copyright is purchased, but that would be on an individual basis when it makes the publication of a book more feasible.

6
Assistance with Publishing

As repeated over and over, DayStar Publishing Company is a **publishing** company rather than a printing company. It is our desire to see that the written works of Bible-believing authors have access to the general Christian public through mainstream bookstores.

Before this happens, a book must be approved by DayStar for publication. This approval **must** be secured by the author **before** the book is printed.

How do I get my book approved?

Submitting a manuscript copy

If you are interested in having DayStar Publishing publish your book, you will be required to submit a **typed** copy in manuscript form. This manuscript will become the property of DayStar Publishing and will not be returned to the author. **But** under no circumstances does the submission of a manuscript constitute the surrender of your copyright to DayStar. The paper and ink copy you send will be our property, but the right to copy the words of that text will be exclusively yours. The only exception to this is for any additional copies that may be reproduced in house for our various readers. None will be copied for resale.

This manuscript is to be a facsimile of the finished, formatted book, not a rough draft copy. It should have already been proofread and contain page headers, page numbers, and your choice of fonts. Your manuscript copy must also include all opening and closing pages that will be in your finished book.

For the purpose of securing ISBN and Library of Congress numbers, if your book is approved for publication, DayStar Publishing will need to know the exact number of pages it will have. This **cannot** be determined from a rough draft. We will also wish to review your typesetting for visual qualities and readability.

This manuscript will then be reviewed by DayStar. The objective of DayStar Publishing is to influence the **uninformed** Christian public concerning the correctness of the King James position. We wish to supply mainstream bookstores with materials that will educate their clientele in this crucial issue. Therefore, books whose main thrust is to berate and divide the Bible-believing group will not be accepted for publication. If you have an ax to grind with a fellow Bible believer, you will have to grind it somewhere else. If you have a personal doctrine to declare, you will want to look elsewhere.

However, the denial of publication for one title does not necessarily assure the denial of publication of a different work that is written by that same author but which addresses a different subject. It is simply our intention to be used as a vehicle to further a worthy cause rather than a power base for a small-minded tyrant to cause damage to that cause.

Submitting a floppy or CD

DayStar also **requires** that you submit a computer disk with the entire text of your book. This will assist us in the approval process. Again, this disk copy will only be copied for in-house needs.

This disk is to be in either the Microsoft Word or Corel WordPerfect word processing programs.

Submitting cover graphics

At the time you submit the manuscript and disk copies of your book, you will also be required to submit a color copy of your cover. This copy must be the same size as it will be on the book. It must include front, back and spine views.

What happens if my book is approved?

If your book is approved for publication, you will be informed of DayStar's decision. DayStar may make suggestions concerning wording or other relevant areas of your book that will enhance its chance of selling.

Upon receipt of notice of acceptance, you will then decide if you wish to have DayStar publish your book. If a book is approved for publication, **you** still make the final decision on whether you wish to work through DayStar Publishing.

If you determine that you wish to have DayStar publish your book ,you will advise DayStar Publishing of your decision. At that time we will begin the process of securing ISBN and Library of Congress numbers for your book.

Upon obtaining these numbers, DayStar will send you a camera ready author's title page with the DayStar logo secured to it and a copyright page with your assigned ISBN and Library of Congress numbers. These sheets are to be inserted in the proper position in the camera ready manuscript you will be sending your printer.

What next?

Re-approval

The next step to be taken is the printing of your book. Following receipt of the author's title page and copyright pages from DayStar, you are now cleared to send your book to the printer of your choice. For the suggested number of copies to be printed, see Part 1, Chapter 2, "Printing Your Book."

Upon the completion of the printing of your book, you will submit **two finished copies** to DayStar Publishing along with a signed form assuring that no changes have been made to the text that had been previously approved.

It is unfortunate but true that there are many unscrupulous people in the world. Saved people? Yes, unscrupulous **"saved"** people. **"King James Bible-believing"** unscrupulous people? Yes, saved, King James Bible-believing people who are so crooked that when they die they will have to be screwed into the ground! It would not be beneath such people to submit a manuscript, get it approved, and then make unacceptable changes to it before getting it printed and slipping it in under the previous approval. For that reason, a copy of the finished book will be compared

Assistance with Publishing

page-by-page with the manuscript copy you previously submitted for **final** approval. Any changes in spelling or grammatical changes will be taken into consideration. But if unacceptable changes have been made, the book will be rejected and not published. It will not be placed in the DayStar Publishing catalog for distribution to bookstores. No copies will be purchased for distribution by DayStar. The DayStar logo on the Author's Title Page **will have to be covered over** before the individual books can be sold. Although you may own the copyright to your book, the DayStar logo is **exclusive property** of DayStar Publishing and cannot be used without **final** approval of your **printed** book.

Into the DayStar Publishing catalog

Upon its **final** approval, your book will be cleared to be added to the DayStar Publishing catalog with a brief synopsis of its contents. This will be written by you and may be edited to fit into the catalog.

The catalog is the primary vehicle used to inform bookstores of the existence of your book. It is the objective of DayStar to place copies of this catalog in the hands of managers of as many mainstream bookstores as possible. Once the catalog is in their possession, it will be the cover art, the synopsis, and **the Lord** that determine if the bookstore will carry your book.

Catalogs will be mailed and hand-delivered to bookstores. Copies will be made available to anyone interested who wishes to hand-deliver copies to bookstores in his area.

7
Assistance with Distribution

As part of its service as the publisher of your book, DayStar Publishing will also act as the primary distributor of your book. We did not say "exclusive" distributor of your book. Such an arrangement would limit your ability to market your book personally, thus denying you opportunities for sales other than through DayStar.

DayStar's part in distribution

Distribution to bookstores

Upon the completion of the printing of your book, DayStar Publishing **will not** purchase the entire printing. Since no one can know how well a book will sell, it would be financial suicide to arbitrarily purchase every book printed and then have them languish in some warehouse until the Lord returns. Instead, we will make an initial purchase of your book so that we will be able to fulfill requests for it made by bookstores and individuals due to catalogs, advertisements, or other venues of exposure. It will be required by you that, as long as printed copies exist, DayStar Publishing will always be supplied **first** with all requested copies before any other requests are fulfilled by you.

As your primary distributor, DayStar Publishing will purchase books at the distributor's discount. (See Part 1, Chapter 2.) These books will be sold to bookstores at a 40% discount or in some cases sent free in attempts to interest them in purchasing your book.

As DayStar's stock of your book is depleted, more will be purchased in proportion with its demand by bookstores.

Individual sales

In addition to its catalog, DayStar Publishing has a limited ability to market books individually. This can increase the chance for the sale of your book. DayStar Publishing makes no promise to individually market every book that it approves for publishing.

Your part in distribution

As stated earlier, it is **not** the intention or desire of DayStar Publishing to maintain a stranglehold on the distribution rights to your book. We will always be recognized as your **primary** distributor but not your **exclusive** distributor. If we were your exclusive distributor, it would limit the marketing of your book. Since we will not be the exclusive distributor of your book, you will be free to market your book in any way you wish through local bookstores, avenues of advertising, or any other means that presents itself. DayStar Publishing would realize **no profit**, nor would it demand any from the sale of books that are not sold through its efforts. This **greatly** expands your opportunities to market your book. Why does DayStar not seek exclusive rights to market your book? Because the **primary** goal of DayStar Publishing is not control or making money. The primary goal of DayStar Publishing is the dissemination of the information contained in your book. Thus, by not restricting your own personal efforts to market your book, DayStar Publishing is attempting to utilize all avenues of distribution for your book, even if it does not profit from them.

It should be obvious that DayStar Publishing would have far more contacts for prospective sales than the average individual. That is why it is to your advantage to have your book approved, published, and distributed by DayStar. But DayStar further recognizes that there will be certain markets or individuals that it cannot reach. This is where your individual efforts will not be discouraged.

Flexibility first

Times change and so do market opportunities. Therefore DayStar Publishing will always be ready to alter its operating structure to function effectively. There may be cases where individual books will receive special considerations and working relations. Though these remain unseen now, DayStar Publishing does not want to restrict or limit its ability to successfully publish the books of its clientele.

8
What Should You Do Now?

Start writing!

If you have a desire to communicate your thoughts in book form, you should begin right now. Investigate your subject. Prove your thesis clearly and **honestly**. Do so without ranting and raving. The less sure a person is of his position, the louder he yells. Although this style may be effective in Marine Corps boot camp, it does little to prove one's point.

Contact DayStar Publishing

After you have written your book and had it proofread and typeset, send a copy to DayStar Publishing for review. If your book is approved, we will send you an ISBN number, a Library of Congress number and the DayStar logo for your title page. Once the book is printed we will do all we can to **publish** it for you.

Don't Contact DayStar Publishing

Do not contact DayStar Publishing until the above steps have been completed in the process of printing your book. It is a sad fact that some people are dreamers. They **dream** great dreams but never quite seem to see them through to reality. These people always possess an infectious zeal for their projects but seldom follow through. The steps mentioned in the preceding paragraph do indeed constitute a few small hurdles. But they are all hurdles you will have to clear before you ever get a book printed, whether you get it published by DayStar or not. Anyone who seeks a shortcut is probably a lazy dreamer who will only consume the limited time and efforts of the DayStar staff. If you don't have a camera-ready manuscript, then stay home and color. Don't call us. We won't call you.

If you're not an author

DayStar Publishing is always looking for qualified personnel to help with the workload of helping authors get their works into mainstream bookstores. If you think you can help in any way feel free to contact DayStar.

If you wish to request some DayStar Publishing catalogs so that you can distribute them among the Christian bookstores in your area feel free to contact DayStar and we will determine how many you need and how we can help.

A Worthy Cause

Anyone who does **anything** feels that his cause is "worthy." Whether it is saving the cobblestones along the New England coast or manufacturing a light bulb that will last for fifty years; it is considered a "worthy cause", **not** because it is, but because **he** are associated with it.

The cause of the Lord Jesus Christ is the greatest of "worthy" causes. That God has provided a **perfect** Bible, free of errors, is a cause that commands our attention. Anyone who works to further that cause will find in Eternity that his efforts **were not** wasted. It is certainly more important than a "Most Improved Score" bowling trophy or a living room that looks like a picture out of Country Living magazine.

We here at DayStar Publishing are certainly sparing no effort or expense to promote the cause of God's perfect Book. If you wish to be a part of such an effort, come and see what you can do.

Appendix

When the first edition of *An Understandable History of the Bible* was printed in 1987 it was a standard sized book, page size was 8.5" x 5.5". There were 242 pages from Chapter One to the end of the footnotes (actually **end**notes) plus about five unnumbered pages for a loose total of about 250 pages. There were 257 foot (**end**) notes. The text font was Times New Roman, size 12. This format lasted through five printings.

When the second edition was printed the book had grown considerably. I had read approximately fifteen additional sources for added material. The book had grown four indices, a second introduction and an entire new chapter in addition to the expansion of existing chapters. Page size was increased to 9.75" x 6.75". Furthermore, there were now approximately 485 total pages with 424 footnotes. And they were indeed **foot**notes, placed right at the foot of each page where the reference was made. The text font was still Times New Roman but the first paragraph of each chapter was size 14. After that it was reduced to size 13. This made for easier reading.

In addition to the three separate indices, the Table of Contents was greatly expanded so that it could be used as a rudimentary index. On the following pages you will find the tables of contents from both editions. The first shown is from the first edition. The second, which has been reduced to 8.5" x 5.5" format (with great difficulty!) for this book is from the second edition. You will see how it is much more useful to the reader. This would be especially true if the second edition had not included any dedicated indices.

Table of Contents

Preface i

Introduction ii

Chapter 1. Time Trip 1

Chapter 2. Where Do We Go From Here 9

Chapter 3. The Ground Rules 15

Chapter 4. The 100 Year War 28

Chapter 5. The Localities 48

Chapter 6. The Witnesses 60

Chapter 7. The Enemy 80

Chapter 8. Westcott and Hort 116

Chapter 9. The Authorized Version 169

Chapter 10. Vindication 219

Bibliography 223

Footnotes 226

Contents

Preface..i

Introduction..ii

Introduction to the Second Edition.......................................v

Chapter 1. Time Trip..1
    Where Is God?..2
    The Communication!...3
    The Questioner...5
    Back Home...6
    The Questioner Returns..7

Chapter 2. Where Do We Go From Here..........................9
    The Questioner...11
    We Have Proof!..11
    My Conversion...12
    What A Book!..13

Chapter 3. The Ground Rules..15
    Why inspire A Book?...17

Appendix

God's Mistake?..21
Rule #1...22
The Power Of Our God........................22
Rule #2...24
The Great Counterfeiter.......................24
God's Warning......................................27
Satan's Desires......................................28
God's Three Gifts..................................29
The Rules Reviewed..............................31

Chapter 4. The 100 Year War.............33
Revolution..37
Do We Have A Perfect Bible?..............38
The Problem?..40
The Problem!...42
The Shot Heard 'Round The World....44
The Battle For England........................44
Blind Rage!..48
The Real Enemy....................................49
The Test..50
   1. Did God inspire His Word perfectly in the original autographs?................50
   2. Did God promise to preserve His words perfectly throughout history?........53
The "Dumb God" Theory.....................55
The Common Language......................56
Hebrew, God's Divine Choice.............56
Greek, God's Divine Choice................57
English, God's Divine Choice..............57
The Development Of English..............59
The Archaic Con-Job...........................63

Read The Book!..66

Chapter 5. The Localities..69
Family Feud..69
The Beginning..71
Egypt...73
Alexandria...76
Dangers Of Ignoring The Bible's Warnings......78
The Alexandrian Mentality................................80
Syria..81
Antioch..81
Our Antioch..82
God's Move...83
    The Alexandrian Mentality........................86
    The Antiochian Mentality.........................86

Chapter 6. The Witnesses..88
Defining The Terms...89
1. The Copies..90
    A. Minuscules...90
    B. Majuscules or Uncials.........................92
    C. Cursives...93
    D. Lectionaries..94
2. The Versions...95
3. The Church Fathers...................................96
The Text: Problems With Transmission.............98
The Editor: Defining The Text........................100
Erasmus: The Greatest Of Editors...................107
Taking Sides...112
The Good Guys..113

Appendix

The "Original" Vulgate 116
Crooked Tactics 117
The Bad Guys 118
Witness From Egypt 119
False Witness From Rome 122
The Local Mess 125
Total Corruption 126

Chapter 7. The Enemy 132
Invasion! 134
The Plot 138
Counterattack 140
The Diabolical Jesuits 142
The Devil's Plainclothesmen 143
Holy Murder 145
The Gunpowder Plot 149
A New Plan 152
The Dreaded Happening 154
Aiding The Enemy 154
Ripe For Conquest 158
"Operation Undermine" 158
Science "Falsely So-called" 159
The Greek Game 163
Griesbach 167
The Puppeteer 170
The Puppets 171
The Oxford Movement 172
Agents Of Apostasy 185
    1. Exalting Men 186
    2. Changing Terminology 187
    3. "Breaking Down the Walls" 188

        A. Doctrine..................................189
        B. Standards................................189
        C. The King James Bible................190
Where We Stand....................................191

Chapter 8. Westcott and Hort.........................192
    A Monumental Switch........................193
    Vicious Prejudice............................194
    A Shocking Revelation......................196
    Blatant Disbelief.............................197
    Strange Bedfellows..........................199
    Forsaking Colossians 2:8...................201
    Lost In the Forest...........................201
        Hort's "Devil"...........................202
        Hort's "Hell"............................202
        Hort's "Purgatory".....................203
        Hort's "Atonement"...................204
        Hort's "Baptism".......................206
        Hort's Twisted Belief.................207
    Problems With Westcott....................212
        Westcott's "Heaven"..................214
        Westcott's "Newmanism".........................215
        Westcott's Defenders..................217
        Westcott's Socialism..................217
        Westcott's Poetical Influences..................220
        Westcott's Romanism.................221
        Westcott's Iconism....................224
        Westcott's Purgatory.................226
        Westcott's Mariolatry................230
        Westcott's Communal Living....................231
        Westcott's Peace Movement......................235

Appendix

Westcott's Faith 239
Westcott's Trepidation 240
Brooke Foss Westcott...Lost! 243
Hort's Fiction 245
Scholarly Prejudice 248
Freedom. Then Slavery 251
The Trap Is Set 252
Scholarly Deceit 254
Defending An Infidel 255
Mission Accomplished 259

Chapter 9. The Authorized Version 261
Inspiration vs Preservation 263
Put Up or Shut Up 263
Unwilling Allies 264
Sowers of Discord 265
Many Shall Come 266
Better Than the Model T! 266
The Super Sack Philosophy 268
The "Super Sack" Version 269
The Sales Pitch 270
The Big Let Down 271
Devastating Revelations 273
Common Complaints 276
The Scholarly Scam 280
Genuine Scholarship 282
    Lancelot Andrews 284
    John Overall 286
    Hadrian Saravia 288
    John Laifield 289
    Robert Tighe 289

William Bedwell..................................289
Edward Lively....................................291
Lawrence Chaderton...........................291
Francis Dillingham..............................293
Thomas Harrison................................294
John Harding......................................294
John Reynolds....................................294
Richard Kilby.....................................296
Miles Smith..298
Henry Saville.....................................298
"Revised" Scholarship..........................299
Edgar Goodspeed................................301
Julius Brewer......................................304
Henry Cadbury...................................304
Walter Bowie......................................304
Clarence Craig....................................305
Frederick Grant...................................306
William Sperry....................................307
William Irwin......................................307
Fleming James....................................308
Millar Burrows....................................309
Modern Scholarship..............................310
Dan Wallace.......................................310
James White.......................................312
Bob Ross..313
Don Wilkins.......................................315
Arthur Farstad....................................317
Kenneth Barker..................................318
Jack Lewis...321
Kurt Aland...323
The King James Apocrypha..................329

Appendix

The Greek Game In Action..................................331
The Greek Game In Reverse............................332
    1. Mark 1:2..334
    2. Luke 24:51..336
    3. Luke 24:52..337
    4. 2 Timothy 2:15......................................338
    5. James 5:16..339
    6. John 9:35..340
More Than Doctrine..342
    1. 1 Samuel 13:1..343
    2. Luke 14:5..344
    3. Luke 23:33..345
    4. Isaiah 14:12..346
    5. 2 Timothy 3:3..347
    6. Galatians 5:12......................................347
    7. Judges 1:14..349
    8. Psalm 23..349
What About The New Scofield Version?..............350
Virtue, Not Fanfare..351
The Counterfeits..352
The ASV "Bust"..353
The NIV Scam..354

Chapter 10. The "King" of the King James Bible
....356
    "James the Kind"..359
    "James the Remarkable"..................................361
    "James the Christian"......................................367
    "James the Incomparable"................................373
        1. United England, Ireland & Scotland......374

    2. Commissioned the King James translation..374
    3. Established the first colony in the New World..374
    4. Desired jury trials................................376
    5. Exalted womanhood & marriage...........376
Who Can Be Against Us?......................................379
    1. The Roman Catholic Church..................380
    2. Opponents of the monarchy....................381
    3. Anti-Scottish racists...............................381
        1. Anthony Weldon........................382
        2. Frances Osborne.........................383
        3. Edward Peyton...........................384
What Do They Hope To Gain?..............................385
    1. The Roman Catholic Church...................386
    2. Marriage & morality haters.....................386
    3. Anti-monarchy/anti-colonialists...............386
    4. The haters of America's Christian heritage..387
    5. The anti-King James Bible crowd...........388
    6. You...389
        1. Distaste for the monarchy............390
        2. Our desire to hear trash.................390
        3. The spirit of the age.....................390
            A. kissing.............................391
            B. Same sex bed sharing.......391
            C. Terms of friendship........392
                a. "gay"..........................392
                b. "parts".........................393
                c. "making love"............393
                d. "terms of friendship".394

Appendix

The Courts of Praise 396
    1. Public reaction 396
    2. Public outcry 396
    3. Puritan cooperation 397
    4. The Anglicans 397
    5. The Bible translator 397
    6. The Colonists 397
    7. God 398

Chapter 11. Considerations, Conclusions & Vindication 399
    Us & Them 400
        1. The Roman Catholic Church 401
        2. They've been wrong before 401
        3. Internal vs external evidence 402
        4. Man vs God 402
        5. "Doctrines found elsewhere" 403
        6. Personal involvement 404
        7. Who are the "Bad Guys"? 405
        8. Revisionist history 407
        9. The rude and the crude 407
        10. The "Common" argument 408
        11. Doing the devil's work 408
        12. What if we're wrong 410
    Your Friends, God's Friends 410
    Apples OR Oranges 414
    The End Result 415
    What Is The Conclusion Of The Matter? ... 416

Appendix A 420

Appendix B..**421**

Bibliography..**422**

Indices..**427**
    Scripture References..427
    Individuals...431
    General...441
    Modern English Versions..................................471

Index

20% 50, 51
40% 49-51, 74
5,000 .... 37, 43-46, 53
500 .... 44, 45, 48
60% 50

A

Adam 29
advertising 16, 48, 49, 74
Americans 33
Answer Book 34
Appendix 20, 21, 79, 92
approval 48, 64, 67, 69-71
approved 59, 61, 64, 65, 67-70, 75, 76
author 2, 5, 11, 13, 20, 24, 27, 29, 32, 33,
                                        49, 50, 55, 57, 58, 60, 67, 68,
                                        77
Author's Title Page 19, 20, 65, 70, 71
automatically 6, 17-19, 27, 41, 66
ax 68

B

Bank 59

bar code 24, 26, 27
bedroom 5
benefit 2, 3, 21, 38, 58, 61
bestow 6
Beverly Hillbillies 10
Bible 3, 8, 12, 22, 29, 32-34, 54-58, 61,
62, 67, 68, 70, 77, 79, 83, 86,
89-91
Bible believers 54-57, 62
Bibliography 21, 81, 92
binding 39
book 1-5, 7, 10-35, 37-51, 53, 54, 59-62,
64-71, 73-80, 82-84
booklet 38, 39
bookstore 18, 24-26, 30, 44, 46, 48-51, 53,
55, 57, 58, 71
Bowker 25, 65
bubble jet 38

C

camera 15, 42, 70, 77
camera ready 15, 42, 70
carnal 32
catalog 55-57, 64, 71, 74
categories 11
CD 13
centered 10, 15, 17
centers 11
chapter headers 16, 17
chapter titles 13, 16, 40
charge 2, 25, 26, 28, 46

Index

Christianity 29
clientele 68, 75
commentaries 3
common 7, 83, 87, 91
communist 32
company 12, 20, 21, 25, 31, 37, 45, 53-57, 59, 64, 67
computer 8, 13, 17, 23, 24, 26, 38-40, 69
Con 35, 36, 51, 84
Conglomerate 60
contact 27-29, 42, 51, 64-66, 76, 77
control 9, 33, 61, 66, 75
copies 31, 38, 39, 42, 43, 45, 46, 48, 53, 67, 69-71, 73, 84
copy right 27
copyright 20, 27, 28, 61, 65-67, 70, 71
Copyright Page 20, 65, 70
Corel 69
cost 24, 30, 39, 45, 47-50, 65
Cover Design 4, 23
crime 4

D

data 9
DayStar 12, 22, 52-54, 56-71, 73-78
decreed 9
Dedication 20
degradation 5
depraved 5
dictionary 7
discounts 49, 50

-95-

distributer 51
distribution 51, 62, 71, 73-75
document 12, 19, 22
doomed 58
draft 39, 40, 68
dream 42-45, 59, 76
dreamers 4, 76

E

Ecclesiastes 33
educational 2, 3
endnotes 12, 79
English 7, 10, 13, 83, 84, 92
environment 3
equation 12, 46, 47, 49, 60
estimates 45
even 7, 9, 16, 18, 23, 24, 27, 29, 32, 39,
44-47, 61, 62, 75
example 12, 21, 47, 48, 61
exclusive 61, 65, 66, 71, 73-75
expense 28, 53, 59, 60, 78
explanation 7, 20, 22

F

fabricators 4
fantasy 4, 43
fiction 4, 43, 57, 87
file 17-19, 22, 23
film laminated 25
filth 5

financial	24, 25, 35, 44, 59, 61, 73
fire	5
first sheet	19
Flexibility	75
font	11-14, 16, 18, 79
fonts	13, 22, 40, 68
footnotes	11, 12, 79, 81
full	11, 49, 58
Fuller	29, 55

G

gamble	31
garbage	5
Gipp	12, 22
give-aways	48
glue	39
God	5, 33, 36, 77, 82, 83, 91
gold	42
grammar	8-10
grammatically	8, 10
grants	27
graphics	4, 23, 42, 69
greedy	32, 62
Guarantor	60
gurus	9

H

HBO	6
headers	16, 17, 22, 40, 68
Hebrews	8
Hidden Costs	47

historical 4
hope 4, 7, 28-31, 58, 90
humor 5, 6
hurdles 77

I

Ibid 12
incidental 2
Index 20, 22, 23, 41, 80
individual 17, 26, 47, 48, 50, 55, 57, 66, 71, 74, 75
infallible 8
influence 2, 56, 62, 68
informative 2, 3
intelligence 6
intolerant 9
Introduction 20, 21, 29, 79, 81, 82
irreparable 4
ISBN 20, 25, 29, 65, 68-70, 76
italics 12, 13, 21

J

Janet Okey 4
Jesus Christ 77
Jude 8
justification 10, 11

K

King James 54, 55, 57, 61, 68, 70, 86, 89, 90

Index

L

labour 33
language 5, 7, 9, 83
laser 38, 41, 42
layout 14, 15, 40
left 11, 15, 16, 19, 24, 45
Legitimate 4, 20, 57, 60
liberal 9, 10
Library of Congress 20, 26, 28, 29, 65, 68-70, 76
logo 25, 65, 70, 71, 76
Lord 58, 71, 73, 77
Louis L'Amour 4

M

magazine 12, 21, 78
mainstream 54, 55, 57, 58, 64, 67, 68, 71, 77
manuscript 15, 19, 28-31, 37, 40-42, 53, 57, 64, 67-71, 77
margin 3, 11, 15, 47
mental 6
Microsoft 69
millions 31, 43, 47
ministerial 3
misconception 4, 37, 47
money 27, 28, 30-35, 44, 46, 49, 50, 55, 61, 75

-99-

N

Never-neverland 9
News Industry 9
News Media 9
nomenclature 3

O

odd 16, 17
Old English 13
one man show 55
opening 14, 19, 20, 40, 41, 68
option 17, 54
orphan 14

P

page 10-23, 40-42, 65, 68, 70, 71, 76, 79
page numbering 17-19, 21, 40
pious 32
pitfall 6
poem 6
poetry 6, 11, 57
prayer 5, 7
Preface 20, 28, 81, 82
primary 54, 61, 62, 71, 73-75
print 24, 25, 29-31, 33-35, 37, 38, 43, 44,
46-49, 53, 55, 57, 59, 61
printer 15, 24, 38, 39, 41, 42, 70
printing 19, 20, 28, 30, 33-37, 41-47, 49,
53, 57, 59, 61, 64, 66, 67, 70,
73, 76

Index

private 5
Pro 51, 54, 55
profit 31-33, 44, 47, 50, 51, 62, 74, 75
public 4, 8, 27, 37, 38, 51, 53, 54, 57, 58,
60, 61, 67, 68, 91
public education 8
publish 28, 30, 33, 53, 55, 57, 59, 62, 64,
67, 69, 75, 76
publishing 12, 20, 22, 25, 28-30, 32, 33, 37,
38, 45, 52-57, 59-65, 67-71, 73-78
purchase 53, 59, 61, 73, 74

Q
qualified 77
quotation 12, 15, 16

R
reader 2, 5-7, 12-15, 20-24, 40, 80
realism 5
redundant 8
repulsive 6
revisionist 4, 91
Re-approval 70
ridiculous 31, 33
right 2, 3, 11, 15, 16, 23, 27, 32, 33, 35,
41, 43, 44, 47, 67, 76, 79
Roman 13, 14, 19, 20, 79, 90, 91

S
saddle stapled 39

Scripture 8, 9, 22, 56, 92
sex 5, 90
shipping 47, 48
sinful 3, 32, 43
Snickers 34
space 11, 12, 15
Spine 24, 42, 69
storage 45, 48
straight 11
style 3, 10-13, 76
substance 4
success 4, 5, 31, 45, 51, 56
suppress 17, 54
symbols 3

T

technical 7
terminology 3, 86
text 4, 11-13, 15, 17-19, 21-23, 39-41, 67,
69, 70, 79, 84
text box 18
tips 6, 10
Title Page 19, 20, 40, 41, 65, 70, 71, 76
Tom Clancy 4, 30, 49
totally blank 19
transgression 5
type 10-13, 18, 22, 23, 27, 29
tyrant 68

Index

U

understandable 8, 12, 22, 29, 34, 55, 79
unspiritual 32, 33
utilize 75

V

venue 62

W

W. E. B. Griffin 4
Washington 26, 28
widow 14
Word 8-10, 12-14, 16-19, 22, 23, 27, 30,
31, 38, 39, 41, 56, 69, 83
word processing 9, 10, 12-14, 16-19, 22, 23,
38, 41, 69
WordPerfect 38, 69
worshipping 9
writing 2, 4, 6-8, 10, 11, 14, 15, 17, 25,
26, 30, 32-35, 37, 43, 76

Gipp's Understandable History of the Bible

A textbook size book that covers the history of the Bible from its conception, through history and into our hands. Written in a simple to understand manner and easily read format. This is a great book for either a new convert or a seasoned Christian who wishes to gain further knowledge of how we got our Bible.

ISBN: 1-890120-13-8 $19.99

The Answer Book

The 62 questions most asked by King James Bible critics, and their answers. Laid out so the average Christian can answer the attacks.
Great for the college student whose faith is being attacked by his school's faculty.

ISBN: 1-890120-00-6 $6.99

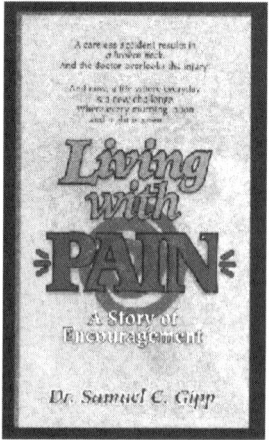

Living With Pain

Samuel C. Gipp, 23 years of age, had recently graduated from Bible college and had entered the field of evangelism. Through an unfortunate accident, which left him with a broken neck, this was postponed for a year. Misdiagnosed he went almost three months before it was surgically corrected. But his ordeal was just beginning. Since that day he has lived a life filled with constant pain. This book has been a great comfort to those who suffer from chronic pain.

ISBN: 1-890120-02-2 $3.99

A Practical and Theological Study of the Book of Acts

Dr. Gipp takes a difficult and sometimes misunderstood book of the Bible and lays it out in an easy to understand manner. The confusion of tongues is dealt with as is the so-called "error" of the translation of "Easter" in Acts 12. A great study help for Bible studies or Sunday School classes.

ISBN: 1-890120-06-5 $19.99

A Practical and Theological Study of the Gospel of John

This study explores the martial skills of the Lord Jesus Christ as He engages and defeats His adversaries time after time. Further subjects are the "wine" of chapter 2 and the authentication for the beginning of chapter 8. A book that will help the teacher as well as the student of Scripture.

ISBN: 1-890120-11-1 $19.99

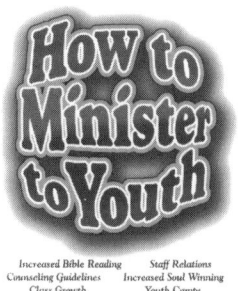

How To Minister To Youth

Dr. Gipp took a problem ridden youth department and built it into a Bible reading, soul winning, dedicated group of young people.

In addition to ideas and instructions on youth camps, banquets, soul winning, and a list of skits and activities, this book tells how to deal with "hard cases" and troubled youth groups.

A must for every pastor and youth group leader

ISBN: 1-890120-07-3 $14.99

Life After Y2K
In this book Dr. Gipp discusses the shameful seven year panic that preceded January 1, 2000. While rebuking Christians for their lack of faith, Dr. Gipp comes down more harshly on the real instigator of the panic, the News Industry.
More importantly, Dr. Gipp tells the reader how to keep from being caught up in the next coming "crisis" which is being planned even now.

ISBN:1-890120-10-3 $3.99

Reading and Understanding the Variations Between the Critical Apparatuses of Nestle's 25th and 26th Editions of the Novum Testamentum-Graece
A technical work to be used with the Nestle-Aland Greek New Testament, suitable for individual or classroom study. This second edition also addresses the changes in the 27th edition of Nestle.

ISBN: 1-890120-16-2 $14.99

Selected Sermons, Vol. 1-10
Each volume in this series highlights five of Dr. Gipp's most requested sermons. Over 30 years of preaching have gone into these works. These messages are still being used of God to His glory.

ISBN:
Volume 1 1-890120-08-1 $14.99
Volume 2 1-890120-14-6   each

Call in your order at: 1-800-311-1823
To order these books or receive a free catalog contact:
DayStar Publishing * PO Box 464 * Miamitown, OH 45041